LEVEL D Foundations

Extreme Weather

Literacy Navigator™

America's Choice

PEARSON

Boston, Massachusetts
Chandler, Arizona
Glenview, Illinois
Upper Saddle River, New Jersey

Copyright © 2012 Pearson Education, Inc., or its affiliate(s). All Rights Reserved. Printed in the United States of America. This publication is protected by copyright, and permission should be obtained from the publisher prior to any prohibited reproduction, storage in a retrieval system, or transmission in any form or by any means, electronic, mechanical, photocopying, recording, or likewise. The publisher hereby grants permission to reproduce these pages, in part or in whole, for classroom use only, the number not to exceed the number of students in each class. Notice of copyright must appear on all copies. For information regarding permissions, write to Pearson Curriculum Group Rights & Permissions, One Lake Street, Upper Saddle River, New Jersey 07458.

America's Choice, the America's Choice A logo, Literacy Navigator, Pearson, and the Pearson Always Learning logo are trademarks, in the U.S. and/or other countries, of Pearson Education, Inc. or its affiliate(s).

PEARSON

ISBN: 978-0-66364-077-5
1 2 3 4 5 6 7 8 9 10   V011   16 15 14 13 12

Table of Contents

Lesson 1
What Is a Natural Disaster? — 1

Lesson 2
Extreme Weather Matrix — 7
Extreme Weather Experience — 10

Lesson 3
Weather vs. Climate — 11
U.S. Climate Regions Map — 13
U.S. Geographical Features Map — 14
Regional Records for Temperature — 15
Cities Map — 24

Lessons 4–5
Tornado! — 25
About Tornadoes Chart — 29

Lesson 6
Birth of a Twister — 31
Birth of a Twister Graphic Organizer — 35
Tornado Alley — 36

Lessons 7–8
Unlocking the Whirlwind's Mysteries — 37
Tornado Scales — 43
Whirlwind's Timeline — 46
Fujita Scales — 47
Witnessing a Tornado — 48

Lesson 9
Recent Natural Disasters — 49
Recent Natural Disasters Chart — 53
Three Disasters — 54

Lesson 10
Wild Weather — 55
Thunderstorm Basics — 59
About Thunderstorms Chart — 63
How Rainclouds Form Graphic Organizer — 64
Stages of a Thunderstorm Chart — 65
Storm News Report — 66

Lessons 11–12
Hurricanes: The Greatest Storms on Earth — 67
Saffir-Simpson Hurricane Scale — 73
About Hurricanes Chart — 74
Hurricane Illustration — 75
Hurricane If/Then Statements — 76

Lesson 13
Hurricane Hazards — 77
Storm Surge Web — 82

Lesson 14
Can Anyone Stop the Waves? — 83
Questions about the Text — 87
What Is This Article Mostly About? — 88

Lesson 15
Chasing the Storm — 89
Hurricane Hunters Chart — 93
Hurricane Advice — 94

Lesson 16
Hurricane Hunters — 95
Restore Vital Hurricane Hunters Aircraft Operations — 97
Pronoun Practice — 100

FOUNDATIONS • EXTREME WEATHER—LEVEL D

Table of Contents

Lessons 17–18
Library Research — 101
Evaluating Websites — 102
Research Notes — 103
Notes on Other Presentations — 104

Lesson 19
Coldest Place—Antarctica — 105
Hottest Temperature—El Azizia, Libya — 109
Coldest and Hottest Places Venn Diagram — 114

Lesson 20
Atacama Desert—The World's Driest Desert — 115
Wettest Place—Cherrapunji, India — 117
Driest and Wettest Places Venn Diagram — 119
Where Would You Rather Live? — 120

Lessons 21–22
Death Valley Weather and Climate — 121
Desert Comparison Chart — 130
Death Valley Timeline — 131
Changing Landscape — 132

Lesson 23
The Dust Bowl — 133
The Dust Bowl Web — 141
Letter from the Dust Bowl — 142

Lesson 24
China's Growing Deserts Are Suffocating Korea — 143
Dust Storms Graphic Organizer — 148

Lesson 25
Blizzard of 1966 — 149
Blizzard of 1966 — 151
Blizzards—1966 and Today — 152

Lessons 26–27
Winter Storms: The Deceptive Killers — 153
Winter Storm Hazards — 169
Being Prepared — 170

Lessons 28–29
Climate Change Basics — 171
Human Connection to Climate Change — 182
Climate and Societies — 183

Lesson 30
Culminating Project — 185
Project Planning Sheet — 186
Argument Rubric for Culminating Project — 187
Written Argument Planning Sheet — 188

My Notes — N1

Credits

Table of Contents

My Notes: A Reader's Comprehension of the Texts

INTRODUCTION	N1

LESSON 1
My Notes on "What Is a Natural Disaster?" — N2

LESSON 2
My Notes on "Extreme Weather Matrix" — N3

LESSON 3
My Notes on "Weather vs. Climate" — N4

LESSON 4
My Notes on "Tornado!" — N5

LESSON 5
My Notes on "Tornado!" — N6

LESSON 6
My Notes on "Birth of a Twister" — N7

LESSON 7
My Notes on "Unlocking the Whirlwind's Mysteries" — N8

LESSON 8
My Notes on "Unlocking the Whirlwind's Mysteries" and "Tornado Scales" — N9

LESSON 9
My Notes on "Recent Natural Disasters" — N10

LESSON 10
My Notes on "Wild Weather" and "Thunderstorm Basics" — N11

LESSON 11
My Notes on "Hurricanes: The Greatest Storms on Earth" — N12

LESSON 12
My Notes on "Hurricanes: The Greatest Storms on Earth" — N13

LESSON 13
My Notes on "Hurricane Hazards" — N14

LESSON 14
My Notes on "Can Anyone Stop the Waves?" — N15

LESSON 15
My Notes on "Chasing the Storm" — N16

LESSONS 16
My Notes on "Hurricane Hunters" and "Restore Vital Hurricane Hunters Aircraft Operations" — N17

LESSONS 17–18
My Notes on Library Research — N18

LESSON 19
My Notes on "Coldest Place—Antarctica" and "Hottest Temperature—El Azizia, Libya" — N19

LESSON 20
My Notes on "Atacama Desert—The World's Driest Desert" and "Wettest Place—Cherrapunji, India" — N20

FOUNDATIONS • EXTREME WEATHER—LEVEL D

Table of Contents

Lesson 21

My Notes on "Death Valley Weather and Climate" — N21

Lesson 22

My Notes on "Death Valley Weather and Climate" — N22

Lesson 23

My Notes on "The Dust Bowl" — N23

Lesson 24

My Notes on "China's Growing Deserts Are Suffocating Korea" — N24

Lesson 25

My Notes on "Blizzard of 1966" — N25

Lesson 26

My Notes on "Winter Storms: The Deceptive Killers" — N26

Lesson 27

My Notes on "Winter Storms: The Deceptive Killers" — N27

Lesson 28

My Notes on "Climate Change Basics" — N28

Lesson 29

My Notes on "Climate Change Basics" — N29

Lesson 30

My Notes on the Culminating Project — N30

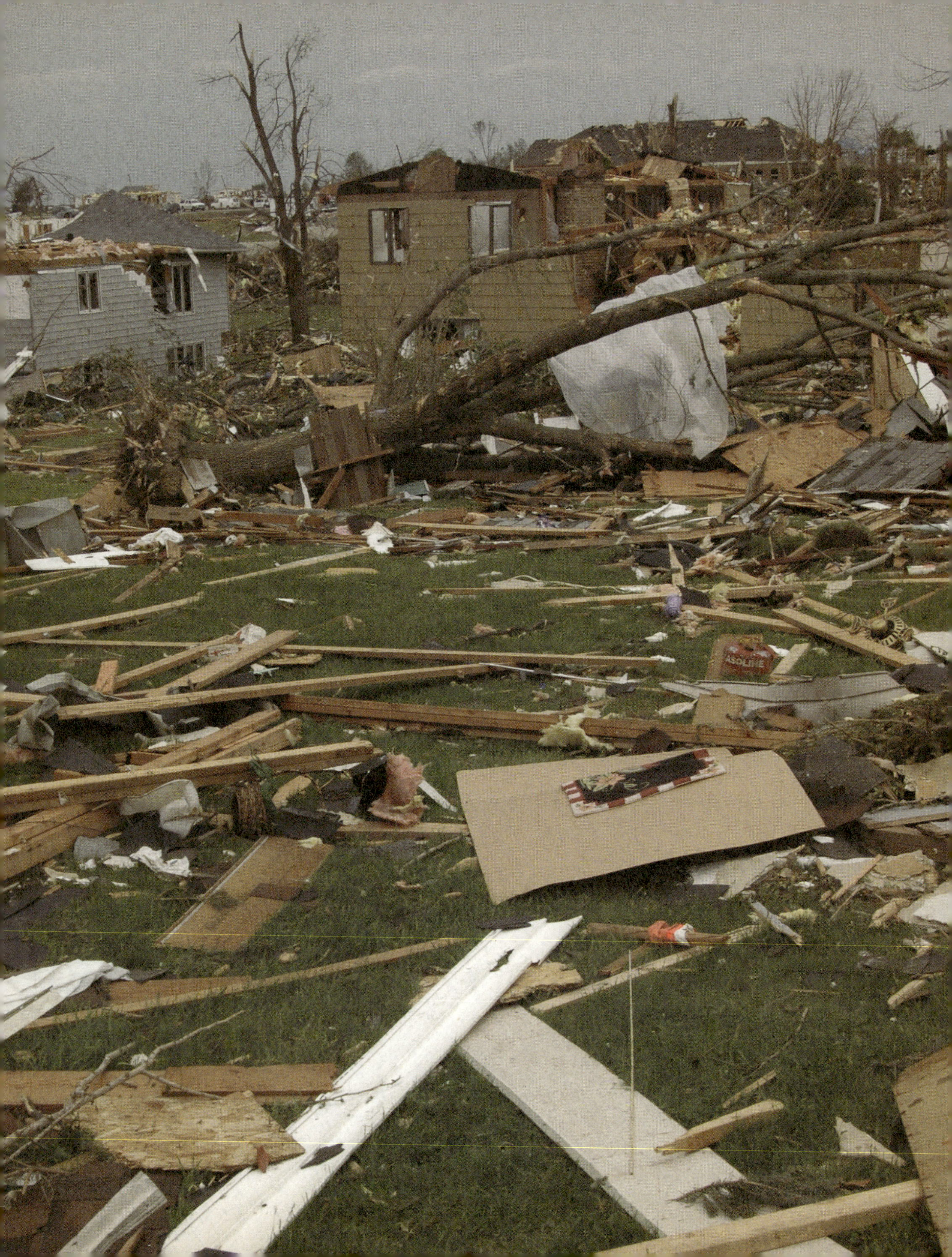

Reading Passage for Lesson 1

What Is a Natural Disaster?

An earthquake-damaged school in Yingxiu, Sichuan, China

1. Earth is a dynamic planet that is always changing—its different parts **simultaneously** breaking down and building up. Volcanoes burst forth from the ocean floor, and mountainous islands grow. **Torrential** rains cause massive mudslides, and cliffs come crashing down. The **storm surge** of a hurricane erodes the shoreline, and flooding has been known to change the course of a river. Severe drought, coupled with wind, can strip the landscape bare and rob soil of its nutrients. West Coast earthquakes rattle and rumble, and by the end of the year, California is three inches closer to Alaska! That's a dynamic Earth—one that can build mountains and move continents.

simultaneously
at the same instant

torrential
pouring in abundance

storm surge
water pushed from the sea onto the land by high winds, usually from a hurricane

Photo: © iStockphoto.com/Youding Xie;
Photo: © iStockphoto.com/David Claassen (left)

FOUNDATIONS • EXTREME WEATHER—LEVEL D

What Is a Natural Disaster?

devastated
caused extensive damage to

innumerable
too many to be counted

2   Any one of these events could be considered a **natural disaster**, a disaster caused by natural rather than human forces that destroys life and property, but on a planetary scale, it's just another typical day on Earth. Some people worry when they tally up the number of disasters that have occurred lately. It's true that the last decade included some extreme weather and Earth events. An earthquake followed by mudslides **devastated** Pakistan, a vicious quake in Sichuan, China killed thousands of school kids, and a cyclone in Burma took 140,000 lives. A tsunami generated by an earthquake in the Indian Ocean killed almost a quarter million people. Almost 2,000 Americans died as a result of Hurricane Katrina, the storm that shattered lives, separated families, and left countless others feeling forgotten and alone. The United States also saw unrelenting flooding and seemingly **innumerable** tornadoes; while Down Under, killer bushfires scorched more than a million acres of Australia's landscape. And just a few months into 2011, Japan experienced a 9.0 earthquake, one of the largest ever recorded. Sooner than the shock could wear off, a tsunami slammed into

Houses lie in rubble three weeks after Hurricane Katrina in Bay St Louis or Waveland, Mississippi.
Photo: © iStockphoto.com/Parker Deen

The Japanese city of Ishinomaki was one of the hardest hit when a powerful tsunami swept ashore on March 11, 2011. Water is dark blue in this false-color image. Plant-covered land is red, exposed earth is tan, and the city is silver.

the country, creating millions of homeless and crippling a nuclear power plant that released harmful amounts of radiation.

Are they happening more often?

3   All that doesn't sound like a typical day on Earth—especially for the people who experience such horrible losses. But Earth has always roared and rumbled, pitched and turned, and stormed itself into a blizzard. The fact is, a large earthquake that is felt only by a few coyote out in the desert is not a disaster at all. It's just an earthquake. And if a colossal tornado roars through an unpopulated area, it is a perfectly natural, though colossal, occurrence of extreme weather but not a disaster. Primarily, it is the proximity of **vulnerable** human populations—and their communities, structures, and livelihoods—that make a powerful weather phenomenon or an extreme Earth event disastrous.

vulnerable
easy to attack or hurt; difficult to defend

Photo: NASA Earth Observatory image created by Jesse Allen, using data provided courtesy of NASA/GSFC/METI/ERSDAC/JAROS, and U.S./Japan ASTER Science Team

What Is a Natural Disaster?

If I'm the only one who feels a large earthquake, is it a natural disaster?

4   Natural disasters will always occur. The effects of these disasters can only be avoided if scientists and warning systems are in place to predict them with accuracy and reliability. As technology has improved, forecasting has improved, making it possible to spot a tropical storm with hurricane potential long before it nears the shore. Even tornado warnings are improving, and that's important when an extra minute can mean the difference between life and death. But other extreme events such as earthquakes are almost impossible to predict.

How do natural disasters affect us?

5   Natural disasters have a huge impact on the human population. Besides taking lives and placing enormous stress on society, in general, natural disasters take an economic toll. They can devastate local communities by wiping out businesses, and require millions of dollars for recovery. Overnight, they can create thousands of homeless and cause entire populations to relocate. They can cause stress, ruin an individual's sense of security, and make it difficult to cope **psychologically**.

> *psychologically*
> mentally; relating to the mind and feelings

Photo: © iStockphoto.com/Todd Burton

6   The word *disaster* is Latin in origin, and the first three letters, *dis*, mean bad or misfortune. But there is some good that comes out of natural disasters. They have inspired invention, goodwill, and growth. Over the years, researchers and scientists have developed new technologies seeking to improve warning systems. Neighbors come together, communities share what resources they have, and countries far away pledge money and support. And usually, societies grow better as they react by creating new policies and better response plans, improving preparedness, and investing in new technology.

Be smart and prepare

7   Natural disasters are a fact of life, so it is important to learn about and understand what types of events can occur in different areas around the country or the world. Besides becoming aware and educating one's self about natural disasters, the other thing to do is prepare. Many people learn about the risks in the area where they live and then keep basic emergency supplies on hand—with water and dried or canned food; basic first aid items and medications; matches, candles, flashlights, even a small generator.

Photo: © iStockphoto.com/Imagesbybarbara

What Is a Natural Disaster?

8   The most important part of preparing for a natural disaster is having a plan. Family members need to know where to meet or where to wait for someone to come for them. Communication devices often fail in times of emergency, so preplanning is key to survival. Some people name a friend or relative outside their area to serve as a common contact. With awareness, preparation, and the help of neighbors and communities, for most of us, weathering the storm will be just another day on active Earth.

Reading Passage for Lesson 2

Extreme Weather Matrix

A thunderstorm in Oklahoma, 2008 (top left); a tornado in Kansas, 2008 (top right); Tropical Storm Bonnie over Florida and the Gulf of Mexico, 2010 (bottom left); Hurricane Irene over the East Coast of the United States, 2011 (bottom right)

All storms are not alike. On the following pages you will find an Extreme Weather Matrix, describing several major storm types, the types of alerts the National Weather Service issues on their behalf, how potentially dangerous they are, and where they are most likely to occur in the United States.

Photos: Sean Waugh NOAA/NSSL (top left and right); NASA/MODIS Rapid Response Team (bottom left); NASA/NOAA GOES Project (bottom right)

Extreme Weather Matrix

	Term	Description	Occurs
1	Thunderstorm	A thunderstorm is a storm with thunder and lightning, often accompanied by rain and sometimes hail. It affects a relatively small area compared to hurricanes and winter storms, being typically about 15 miles in diameter and lasting an average of 30 minutes. All thunderstorms are dangerous. Of the estimated 100,000 yearly thunderstorms in the United States, about 10 percent are considered severe.	March–August States with the most thunderstorms: • 1st: Florida and the Mississippi, Alabama coasts • 2nd: all of Mississippi, Alabama, and Georgia, South Carolina, Tennessee, Arkansas, Louisiana, Missouri, Kansas • 3rd: Tornado Alley (Texas, Oklahoma, Kansas, Nebraska, South Dakota, eastern Colorado), central and north-central states, southwest states
2	Severe Thunderstorm	A severe thunderstorm is a thunderstorm that produces a tornado, winds of at least 58 miles per hour (50 knots), and/or hail at least one inch in diameter. Structural wind damage usually indicates a severe thunderstorm.	
3	Severe Thunderstorm Watch	The National Weather Service (NWS) issues a Severe Thunderstorm Watch to tell people when and where severe thunderstorms are likely to occur. People are advised to watch the sky and stay tuned to know when warnings are issued.	
4	Severe Thunderstorm Warning	The NWS issues a Severe Thunderstorm Warning when severe thunderstorms have been sighted by spotters or detected by radar. A warning indicates **imminent** danger to life and property for those in the path of the storm.	
5	Tornado	A tornado is a violently rotating column of air, usually **pendant** to a **cumulonimbus**, with circulation reaching the ground. It nearly always starts as a funnel cloud and may be accompanied by a loud roaring noise. Average forward speed is 30 mph, but tornadoes can be stationary or move at 70 mph. On average, they move southwest to northeast, but tornadoes have been known to move in any direction. On a local scale, it is the most destructive of all atmospheric **phenomena**.	All United States, but mainly • Early spring: southeast and Gulf states, south-central states • Late spring: Nebraska, Kansas, Missouri, Tennessee • Mid-summer: Tornado Alley • Late summer: Missouri, Iowa, Wisconsin, Illinois, Indiana, Ohio, Kentucky
6	Tornado Watch	The NWS issues a Tornado Watch to alert the public that tornadoes are possible in the watch area. People should know what areas are within the watch area and remain alert for approaching storms.	
7	Tornado Warning	The NWS issues a Tornado Warning to alert the public that a tornado has been sighted by spotters or detected by radar. These warnings indicate where the tornado is presently located and which communities are in its **anticipated** path.	

imminent
about to happen

pendant
a piece of jewelry that hangs from a necklace

phenomena
facts or situations that are observed to exist

anticipated
expected hopefully

LITERACY NAVIGATOR — LESSON 2

Extreme Weather Matrix (continued)

	Term	Description	Occurs
8	Tropical Depression	A tropical depression is a **tropical cyclone** in which the maximum sustained surface wind speed is 38 mph or less.	Warm months: June–November
9	Tropical Storm	A tropical storm is a tropical cyclone in which the maximum sustained surface wind speed ranges from 39 to 73 mph. Each tropical storm is given a name.	• Atlantic Basin: Coastline from Texas to Maine • Northeast Pacific (rare): tend to move west–northwest—well off-shore of United States; west-coast waters too cool to sustain storms
10	Tropical Storm Watch	A Tropical Storm Watch is an announcement that tropical storm conditions (sustained winds of 39 to 73 mph) are *possible* within the specified area within <u>48 hours</u>.	
11	Tropical Storm Warning	A Tropical Storm Warning is an announcement that tropical storm conditions (sustained winds of 39 to 73 mph) are *expected* somewhere within the specified area within <u>36 hours</u>.	
12	Hurricane	A hurricane is a tropical cyclone in the Atlantic and eastern and central Pacific Oceans in which the maximum sustained surface wind speed is greater than 74 mph. Other terms, such as typhoon, are used in other parts of the world to describe the same weather event. Each hurricane is given a name. In the Northern Hemisphere, a hurricane will have a counterclockwise circulation of winds near the Earth's surface.	Atlantic Basin (common origin): • June–November • Peaking August–October Northeast Pacific (rare): • Mid-May–November • Peaking August–September Most hurricanes: Florida 113; Texas 60; Louisiana 52; North Carolina 50; South Carolina 30; Alabama 26; Georgia 23; Mississippi 16; New York 12; Connecticut 11; Massachusetts 12; Virginia 10; Rhode Island 9
13	Hurricane Watch	A Hurricane Watch is an announcement that hurricane conditions (sustained winds of 74 mph or higher) are *possible* within specified coastal or inland areas. Because hurricane-**preparedness** activities become much more difficult once winds reach tropical storm force, the hurricane watch is issued <u>48 hours in advance</u> of the anticipated onset of tropical-storm-force winds.	
14	Hurricane Warning	A Hurricane Warning is an announcement that hurricane conditions (sustained winds of 74 mph or higher) are *expected* somewhere within specified coastal or inland areas. Because hurricane preparedness activities become much more difficult once winds reach tropical storm force, the hurricane warning is issued <u>36 hours in advance</u> of the anticipated onset of tropical-storm-force winds.	

preparedness
a state of being ready for something

Extreme Weather Experience

If you had to choose one weather event listed on the matrix to experience, which one would it be? Why? Write a paragraph explaining your choice. Support your answer with evidence in the text.

Reading Passage for Lesson 3

Weather vs. Climate

1. Weather reflects short-term conditions of the atmosphere, while climate is the average daily weather for an extended period of time at a certain location. We hear about weather and climate all of the time. Most of us check the local weather **forecast** to plan our days. And **climate change** is certainly a "hot" topic in the news. There is, however, still a lot of confusion over the difference between the two.

2. Think about it this way: Climate is what you expect, weather is what you get. Weather is what you see outside on any particular day. So, for example, it may be 75 degrees and sunny or it could be 20 degrees with heavy snow. That's the weather.

forecast
a description of a future condition or occurrence

Photo: Sean Waugh NOAA/NSSL

Weather vs. Climate

3   Climate is the average of that weather. For example, you can expect snow in the Northeast in January or for it to be hot and humid in the Southeast in July. This is climate. The climate record also includes extreme values such as record high temperatures or record amounts of rainfall. If you've ever heard your local weather person say "today we hit a record high for this day," she is talking about climate records.

4   So when we are talking about climate change, we are talking about changes in *long-term* averages of daily weather. In most places, weather can change from minute-to-minute, hour-to-hour, day-to-day, and season-to-season. Climate, however, is the average of weather over time and space.

U.S. Climate Regions

5   The United States is a large and diverse landmass with widely varying climate conditions. Local climates are affected by factors that include **topography**, elevation, proximity to oceans, lakes, and rivers, and latitude. Through climate analysis, National Climate Data Center (NCDC) scientists have identified nine climatically consistent regions within the **contiguous** United States, which are useful for putting current climate **anomalies** into historical perspective.

6   The NCDC climate data have been used in a variety of applications including agriculture, air quality, construction, education, energy, engineering, forestry, health, insurance, landscape design, livestock management, manufacturing, recreation and tourism, retailing, transportation, and water resources management among other areas. Our data and products fulfill needs ranging from building codes to power plant and space shuttle design. Our nation's climate data are critical to our modern lifestyles.

---

contiguous
sharing a boundary or touching each other physically

anomalies
observations or occurrences of things that differ from the norm or what is reasonably expected

U.S. Climate Regions Map

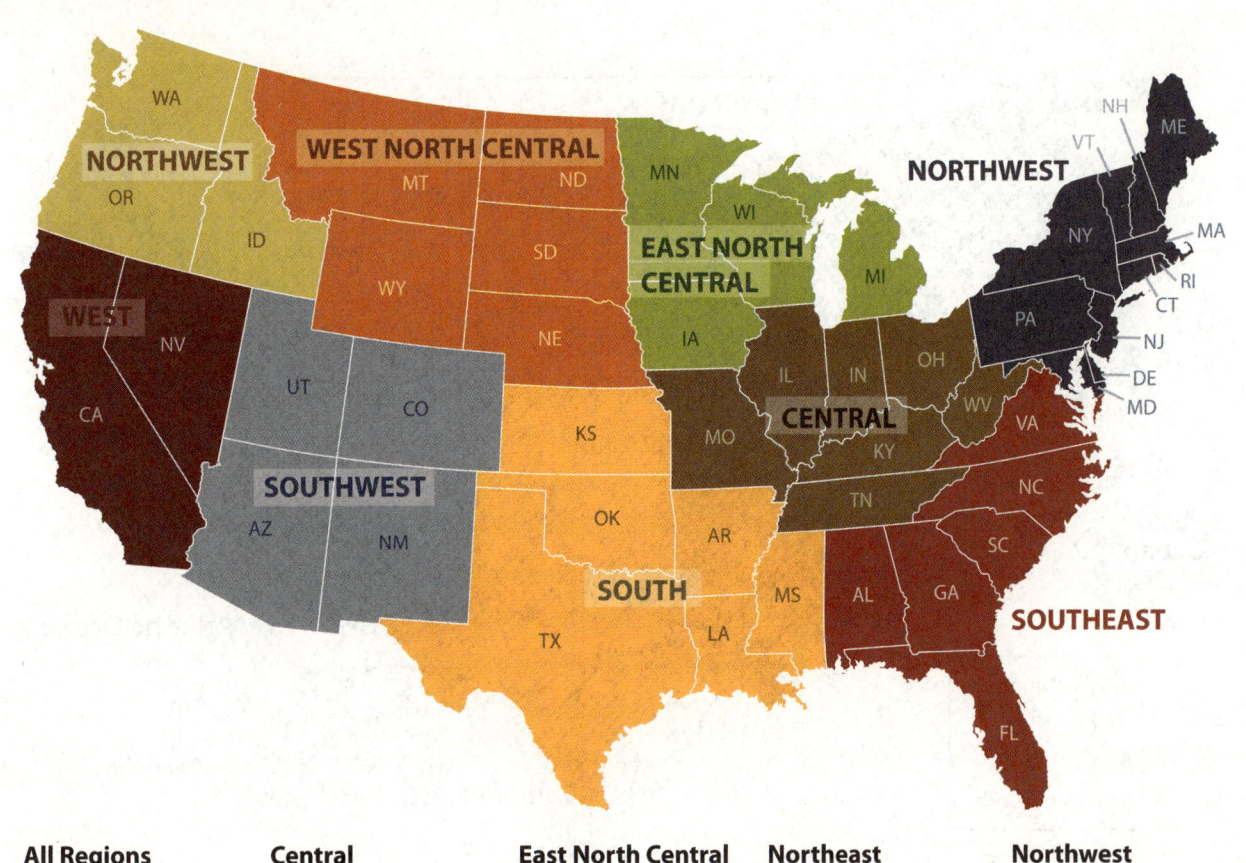

All Regions
Central
East North Central
Northeast
Northwest
South
Southeast
Southwest
West

Central
Kentucky (KY)
Illinois (IL)
Indiana (IN)
Missouri (MO)
Ohio (OH)
Tennessee (TN)
West Virginia (WV)

East North Central
Iowa (IA)
Michigan (MI)
Minnesota (MN)
Wisconsin (WI)

Northeast
Connecticut (CT)
Delaware (DE)
Maine (ME)
Maryland (MD)
Massachusetts MA)
New Hampshire (NH)
New Jersey (NJ)
New York (NY)
Pennsylvania (PA)
Rhode Island (RI)
Vermont (VT)

Northwest
Idaho (ID)
Oregon (OR)
Washington (WA)

South
Arkansas (AR)
Louisiana (LA)
Kansas (KS)
Mississippi (MS)
Oklahoma (OK)
Texas (TX)

Southeast
Alabama (AL)
Florida (FL)
Georgia (GA)
North Carolina (NC)
South Carolina (SC)
Virginia (VA)

Southwest
Arizona (AZ)
Colorado (CO)
New Mexico (NM)
Utah (UT)

West
California (CA)
Nevada (NV)

West North Central
Montana (MT)
Nebraska (NE)
North Dakota (ND)
South Dakota (SD)
Wyoming (WY)

Art: Copyright © Pearson Education, Inc., or its affiliates, adapted from NOAA.

U.S. Geographical Features Map

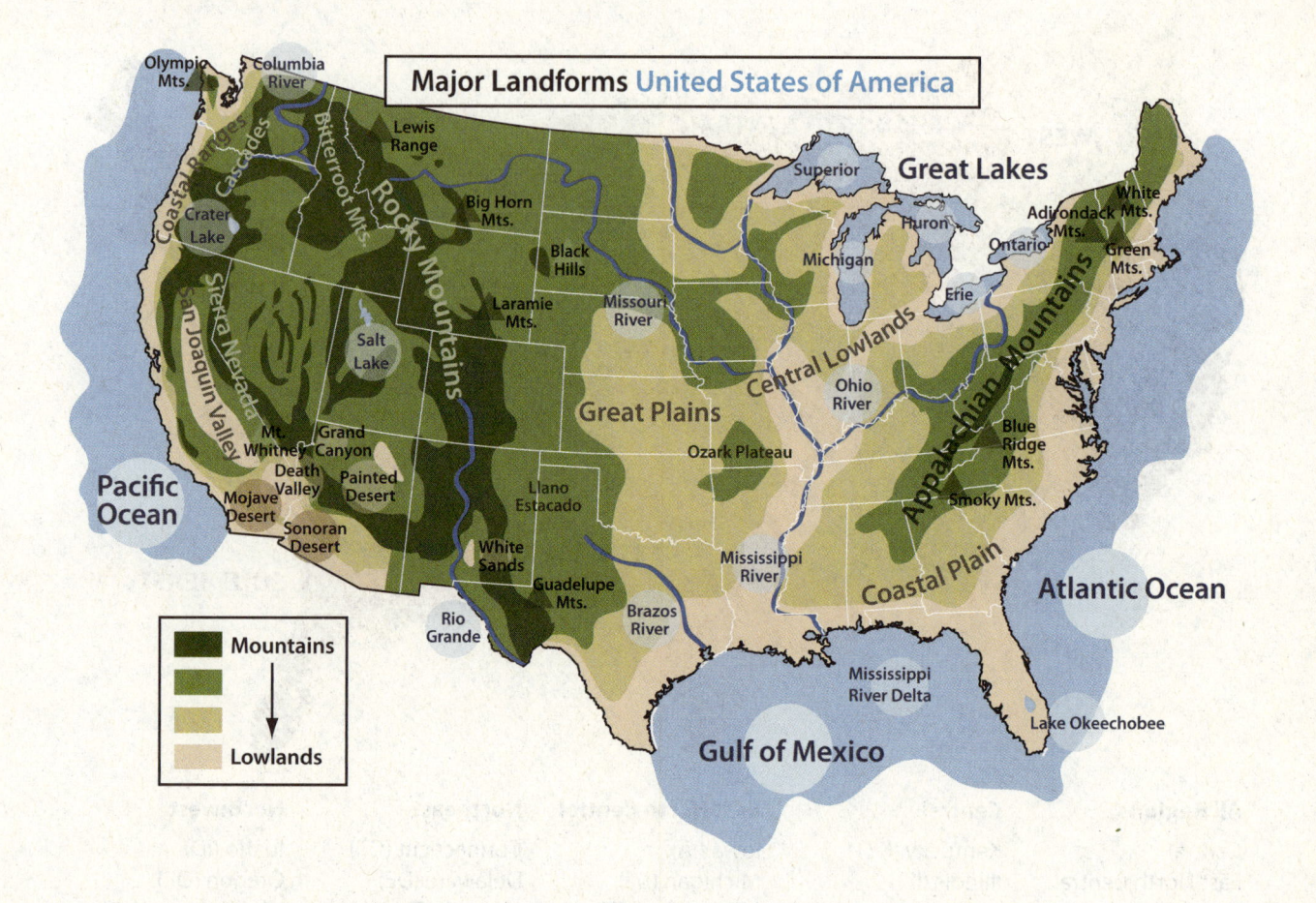

Regional Records for Temperature

West Region

The West region includes the states of California and Nevada.

West Climatic Region	January 15, 2010 High/Low Temperature	July 15, 2010 High/Low Temperature
California		
Los Angeles	69/56	70/64
San Francisco	57/43	77/60
Sacramento	57/40	102/62
Nevada		
Reno	48/28	100/63
Las Vegas	62/39	111/86

Northwest Region

The Northwest region includes the states of Washington, Oregon, and Idaho.

Northwest Climatic Region	January 15, 2010 High/Low Temperature	July 15, 2010 High/Low Temperature
Washington		
Seattle	62/29	75/60
Yakima	56/48	85/45
Oregon		
Portland	55/46	79/57
Bend	50/37	81/45
Idaho		
Coeur d' Alene	15/-6	70/43
Boise	45/30	90/58

Regional Records for Temperature

West North Central Region

The West North Central region includes the states of Montana, Wyoming, North Dakota, South Dakota, and Nebraska.

West North Central Climatic Region	January 15, 2010 High/Low Temperature	July 15, 2010 High/Low Temperature
Montana		
Helena	50/24	81/51
Bozeman	41/19	80/46
Wyoming		
Yellowstone	34/16	86/50
Laramie	28/10	82/53
North Dakota		
Bismarck	41/12	87/53
South Dakota		
Sioux Falls	6/-6	91/68
Nebraska		
Omaha	28/23	89/64
Sidney	48/26	95/59

Regional Records for Temperature

Southwest Region

The Southwest region includes the states of Utah, Arizona, Colorado, and New Mexico.

Southwest Climatic Region	January 15, 2010 High/Low Temperature	July 15, 2010 High/Low Temperature
Utah		
Salt Lake City	39/26	90/64
Bryce Canyon	41/17	82/42
Arizona		
Phoenix	48/30	104/81
Grand Canyon Village	46/15	93/47
Colorado		
Denver	48/28	91/60
Grand Junction	34/7	101/62
New Mexico		
Albuquerque	46/17	91/59
Las Cruces	62/37	97/64

Regional Records for Temperature

South Region

The South region includes the states of Kansas, Oklahoma, Texas, Arkansas, Louisiana, and Mississippi.

South Climatic Region	January 15, 2010 High/Low Temperature	July 15, 2010 High/Low Temperature
Kansas		
Wichita	30/10	104/78
Topeka	34/21	90/71
Oklahoma		
Oklahoma City	36/14	93/71
Tulsa	49/42	96/78
Texas		
Dallas	55/48	97/75
Austin	70/55	95/73
Houston	60/53	97/77
Arkansas		
Fort Smith	60/39	97/78
Little Rock	57/37	96/75
Louisiana		
Shreveport	64/37	95/72
New Orleans	61/38	95/76
Mississippi		
Biloxi	62/55	89/64
Jackson	61/26	99/73

Regional Records for Temperature

East North Central Region

The East North Central region includes the states of Minnesota, Iowa, Wisconsin, and Michigan.

East North Central Climatic Region	January 15, 2010 High/Low Temperature	July 15, 2010 High/Low Temperature
Minnesota		
Hibbing	34/-3	77/54
MInneapolis	32/8	87/62
Iowa		
Cedar Rapids	27/24	88/72
Des Moines	36/26	97/73
Wisconsin		
Green Bay	35/17	84/59
Milwaukee	32/21	78/62
Michigan		
Detroit	54/33	83/64
Sault St. Marie	33/29	78/68

Regional Records for Temperature

Central Region

The Central region includes the states of Missouri, Illinois, Indiana, Ohio, West Virginia, Kentucky, and Tennessee.

Central Climatic Region	January 15, 2010 High/Low Temperature	July 15, 2010 High/Low Temperature
Missouri		
Kansas City	36/23	90/71
St. Louis	53/34	96/79
Illinois		
Chicago	38/28	91/79
Springfield	43/30	93/80
Indiana		
Indianapolis	43/35	92/73
Fort Wayne	36/32	93/72
Ohio		
Columbus	39/35	86/66
Cleveland	42/27	90/65
West Virginia		
Charleston	49/15	91/68
Kentucky		
Louisville	52/41	95/75
Lexington	51/24	90/64
Tennessee		
Memphis	62/30	94/77
Nashville	58/30	94/73

Regional Records for Temperature

Southeast Region

The Southeast region includes the states of Virginia, North Carolina, South Carolina, Georgia, Alabama, and Florida.

Southeast Climatic Region	January 15, 2010 High/Low Temperature	July 15, 2010 High/Low Temperature
Virginia		
Virginia Beach	50/34	87/71
Roanoke	60/25	90/64
North Carolina		
Charlotte	56/34	90/71
Raleigh	63/36	93/64
South Carolina		
Greeneville	66/28	97/79
Charleston	64/37	89/80
Georgia		
Atlanta	57/37	89/71
Savannah	72/52	92/71
Alabama		
Birmingham	58/35	91/70
Mobile	63/35	92/78
Florida		
Jacksonville	66/33	88/71
Key West	74/54	88/76

Regional Records for Temperature

Northeast Region

The Northeast region includes the states of Maryland, Delaware, New Jersey, Pennsylvania, New York, Connecticut, Rhode Island, Massachusetts, Vermont, New Hampshire, and Maine.

Northeast Climatic Region	January 15, 2010 High/Low Temperature	July 15, 2010 High/Low Temperature
Maryland		
Baltimore	45/26	87/66
Delaware		
Dover	54/43	83/62
New Jersey		
Trenton	53/31	83/63
Cape May	43/34	78/75
Pennsylvania		
Pittsburgh	43/23	88/66
Philadelphia	39/22	86/70
New York		
Buffalo	52/40	80/62
New York City	51/35	81/66
Connecticut		
Hartford	38/20	85/62
Rhode Island		
Providence	44/26	79/64
Massachusetts		
Boston	46/28	72/65
Vermont		
Montpelier	43/28	72/57

Regional Records for Temperature

Northeast Climatic Region	January 15, 2010 High/Low Temperature	July 15, 2010 High/Low Temperature
New Hampshire		
Concord	38/20	85/62
Maine		
Portland	42/33	70/64
Augusta	39/19	84/66

Cities Map

Reading Passage for Lessons 4–5

Tornado!

The Hoisington tornado damaged the high school, a small shopping center, the hospital, and hundreds of homes in a matter of minutes.

Photo: FEMA/Dave Saville

1 April 21, 2001, was prom night in Hoisington, Kansas. As kids drove up to the Knights of Columbus Hall, a drizzly rain was falling. After about an hour of dancing, the lights started to flicker on and off. A few minutes later the whole auditorium went dark and the music died. A strong wind sucked the doors open, and the kids could see rain lashing down horizontally. To keep everyone entertained, the DJ found a stick to use as a limbo bar and couples started lining up to duck under it hoping that soon the power would come back on. The high school principal stepped outside to survey the storm just as an ambulance raced down the block. An announcement to take cover blared over the ambulance's public address system. The principal ran back into the hall and shouted for everyone to go down into the basement.

Tornado!

The tornado tore a large hole in the roof of the high school auditorium.

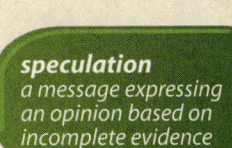

speculation
a message expressing an opinion based on incomplete evidence

chaotic
lacking a visible order or organization

ferocious
violent and able to cause serious damage or injury

2   The kids wanted to know what was going on—maybe a severe thunderstorm or even a tornado? "At this point it would only be **speculation**," the principal told them.

3   Across town at the Dairy Queen, Gloria Adams recalled hearing a frightening roar at about 9:30 at night. "People are describing it as a freight train. I don't know if it sounded like a freight train, it was the most horrible roar I've ever heard in my life."

4   Realizing it was a tornado, the restaurant owner shouted for everyone to hide in the walk-in cooler. Before Adams could get there, the Dairy Queen's roof was yanked away. Debris flew through the restaurant. Napkins whirled like white confetti, boards slammed into the counter, dishes and silverware flew out into the dark **chaotic** night. Adams fell to her hands and knees to try to avoid getting hit. The **ferocious** wind felt like a hand holding her back as she crawled around the corner to huddle with five other employees inside the cooler. "It's not very big," Adams remembered, "this cooler where they keep, oh, like their Dairy Queen toppings for their ice cream and stuff like that."

Photo: FEMA/Dave Saville

5   Clinging to each other in terror, they heard the tornado rip the building apart. "Everyone was just so scared," Adams recalled. "We cried; we yelled; we prayed. God please let us get out of this alive." And then it was all over. The roaring monster was gone. Gloria Adams and the other employees pushed open the cooler door and stared at the rubble. It looked like a bomb had gone off.

6   Across town the kids at the prom were still in the basement, unaware of what had happened outside. Some used their cell phones to call friends and family. One girl recalled that rumors were flying: "All of a sudden someone pops up and says, 'Zack, your house is gone.'... And then it was all of Fifth Street's gone and all of Sixth Street's gone.... There are people crying because we can't leave and we don't know where our families are.... All I could do was cry."

7   When they finally went upstairs, the air was cool and the power was out on Main Street, but otherwise everything looked fine. Police cars, ambulances, and fire trucks sped by, brightening up the night with their flashing red-and-blue lights. Parents started arriving and the kids could tell by their expressions that something awful had happened. One boy said, "I walked up to [my mom] and she started crying and my sister was sitting there crying and I was just like oh no I kind of sat there and I didn't believe it at first.... A tornado. How could there be a tornado without us knowing?"

8   One girl ran home in her prom dress leaping over fallen tree limbs and downed power lines. When she got there, she found the roof had been ripped off her house. More than four hundred homes were either damaged or totally lost, but only one person, an elderly man, died—a remarkable statistic considering that the tornado cut from one end of town to the other, creating a six block, mile-long path of destruction.

Tornado!

telltale
obvious signs that something exists or has happened

9   Every year eight hundred tornadoes strike the United States and, on average, 80 people die and 1,500 people are injured. It is very difficult to predict exactly where and when a tornado will strike. At best, forecasters can say that in the next eight to twelve hours there might be some thunderstorms that might produce one or more tornadoes over a large area that may include a number of different states. An hour or so in advance, scientists can narrow down the region likely to be hit, but they can't say for certain whether or not a tornado will form, how big it will be, and what path it will take. Once the storm starts to show **telltale** rotation or a funnel appears, they can issue tornado warnings that give people, on average, between eleven minutes and half an hour to seek shelter.

More than 400 buildings were damaged or destroyed when a tornado struck Hoisington, Kansas, the night of April 21, 2001.

10 That's not much time, but as recently as 1986, the National Weather Service was providing only four and a half minutes of lead time on its average tornado warnings. The improvement was due in large part to research done by a group of tornado scientists who are hard at work right now in a part of the United States known as Tornado Alley.

Photo: FEMA/Linda Winkler

About Tornadoes Chart

Known about Tornadoes	Learned about Tornadoes

About Tornadoes Chart

Known about Tornadoes	Learned about Tornadoes

Reading Passage for Lesson 6

Birth of a Twister

1. Tornado Alley is a region that roughly **encompasses** the states lying between the Mississippi River and the high plains—mainly Texas, Oklahoma, Kansas, Nebraska, Iowa, Missouri, Arkansas, and Louisiana. Each spring the weather conditions there are perfect for producing the powerful thunderstorms that cause tornado outbreaks. Scientists flock to this area because, while tornadoes occur in many parts of the world and have struck in every state of the union, nowhere on Earth are they as common as in Tornado Alley.

2. Here, from April through June, very warm moist air from the Gulf of Mexico rushes northward where it **encounters** winds blowing in from central Mexico to the southwest. At an even higher altitude, cold winds gust in from the Rockies. Wind shear is the word **meteorologists** use to describe winds that blow in different directions at different altitudes.

Photo: NOAA Photo Library, NOAA Central Library; OAR/ERL/National Severe Storms Laboratory (NSSL)

encompasses
surrounds or includes entirely

encounters
comes upon or meets with, especially unexpectedly

FOUNDATIONS • EXTREME WEATHER—LEVEL D

Birth of a Twister

Tornado Alley

3. Generally, warm air wants to rise. As it does, it encounters the wind shear and starts to rotate. To understand why, imagine making a snake out of clay: You put a ball of clay on one palm and then roll it back and forth between both palms. As you do so, one hand goes away from you while the other hand comes back toward you, and the clay rotates into a snake. Similarly, air will spin in an invisible horizontal tube (a snake shape) when one wind above pushes it going one way and another wind below pushes it going the other.

4. While the air is rotating like this, the sun is also heating the ground, which causes upward-moving currents. The currents eventually jerk the rotating air into a vertical position (so that the snake is standing on its tail).

Art: Copyright © Pearson Education, Inc., or its affiliates.

intensely
in an extreme manner; severely

5   Now this tube of **intensely** rotating air acts like a vacuum hose feeding hot, moist air from the ground up into the higher levels of the atmosphere. As this air rises, it cools and turns into condensation (water droplets). The water droplets make thunderclouds. As more warm air continues to get sucked up, the thunderclouds bubble upward looking like shaving cream mountains in the sky.

A tornado at the beginning of its life—the condensation funnel has not yet reached ground. However, the dust cloud at surface indicates touchdown near Cordell, Oklahoma, 1981.

6   Eventually the clouds will reach an altitude where they can no longer keep rising, usually between 30,000 and 50,000 feet (9,144 and 15,240 meters). At these heights, the cloud tops become filled with ice crystals and snowflakes. These powerful thunderstorms with deeply rotating and long-lived updrafts are called supercells. Supercells will often send hail and lightning slashing to the ground. One tornado researcher recalled driving through such a fearsome hailstorm that both the front and back windshields shattered. "We kept driving anyway," he said. "Little **slivers** of glass were everywhere. My driver got slivers in his face; I got them in my laptop computer while I was typing on it. I put my clipboard against the windshield for some protection."

slivers
small thin pieces of something, often sharp, usually broken off something larger

Photo: NOAA Photo Library, NOAA Central Library; OAR/ERL/National Severe Storms Laboratory (NSSL)

Birth of a Twister

7. In a supercell there is an area of strong rotation called the ***mesocyclone***. Some mesocyclones (though not all) give birth to tornadoes. If a tornado is going to form, several events tend to occur almost simultaneously:

   - The mesocyclone tightens its rotation. The tighter it gets, the faster it spins, in the same way that figure skaters will spin faster when they draw their arms in close to their bodies.

   - Rotating violently, the mesocyclone then moves to the rear of the storm. From the ground, you might see a rotating section of cloud drop from the storm's southwestern base, looking like a boat's rudder. This rudder-shaped cloud is called the rotating wall cloud.

8. Tornado researchers know that the appearance of a wall cloud means that it is show time and tornadoes may start twisting at any minute.

9. While all of this is going on, a clearly defined **cascade** of warm humid air also flows downward from the storm's rear. This is called the Rear Flank Downdraft (RFD). The RFD is strong enough to shake cars, knock down power lines, and send farm equipment tumbling. Tornado researchers call this violent rear area of the storm "the bear's cage" because to get under it can be as deadly as walking into a grizzly bear's cage.

10. Greg Forbes, a severe-weather expert, explained that while scientists don't know all the forces that cause the rotation in the mesocyclone to reach the ground, in general, "thunderstorm downdrafts or other processes allow some of the rotation aloft to reach or develop at the surface. At that point, updrafts can concentrate this low-level rotation into a … tornado."[1]

---

1. "Inside Tornadoes." [Online] Available at: http//www.weather.com/newscenter/specialreprots/tornado/index.html, August 21, 2002.

cascade
something rushing forth or falling in quantity

Birth of a Twister Graphic Organizer

Step ___

Step ___

Step ___

Step ___

Step ___

Step 1

Tornado Alley

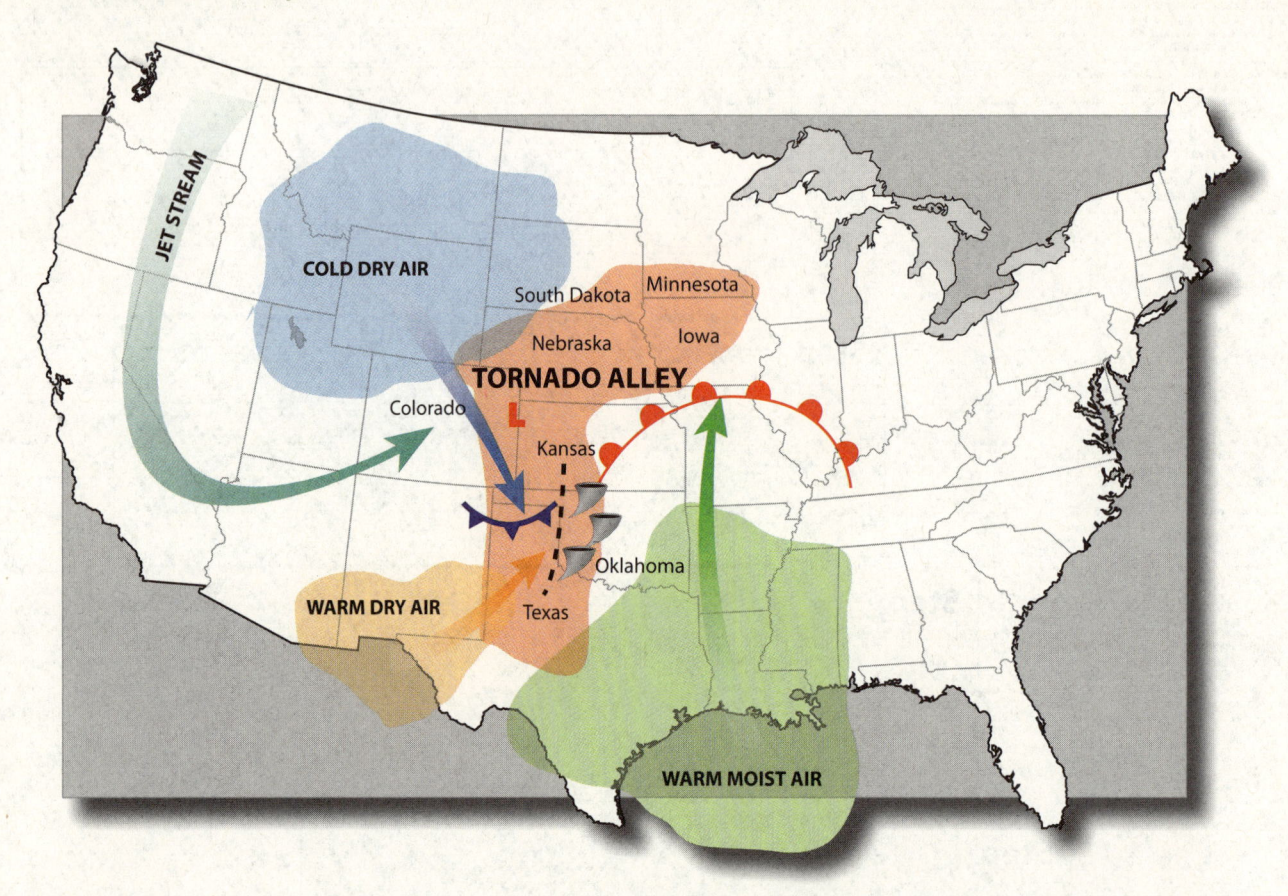

Tornado Alley is a nickname for an area that consistently experiences a high frequency of tornadoes each year. The area that has the most strong and violent tornadoes includes eastern SD, NE, KS, OK, northern TX, and eastern Colorado. The relatively flat land in the Great Plains allows cold dry polar air from Canada to meet warm moist tropical air from the Gulf of Mexico. A large number of tornadoes form when these two air masses meet.

Art: Copyright © Pearson Education, Inc., or its affiliates, adapted from NOAA.

Reading Passage 1 for Lessons 7–8

Unlocking the Whirlwind's Mysteries

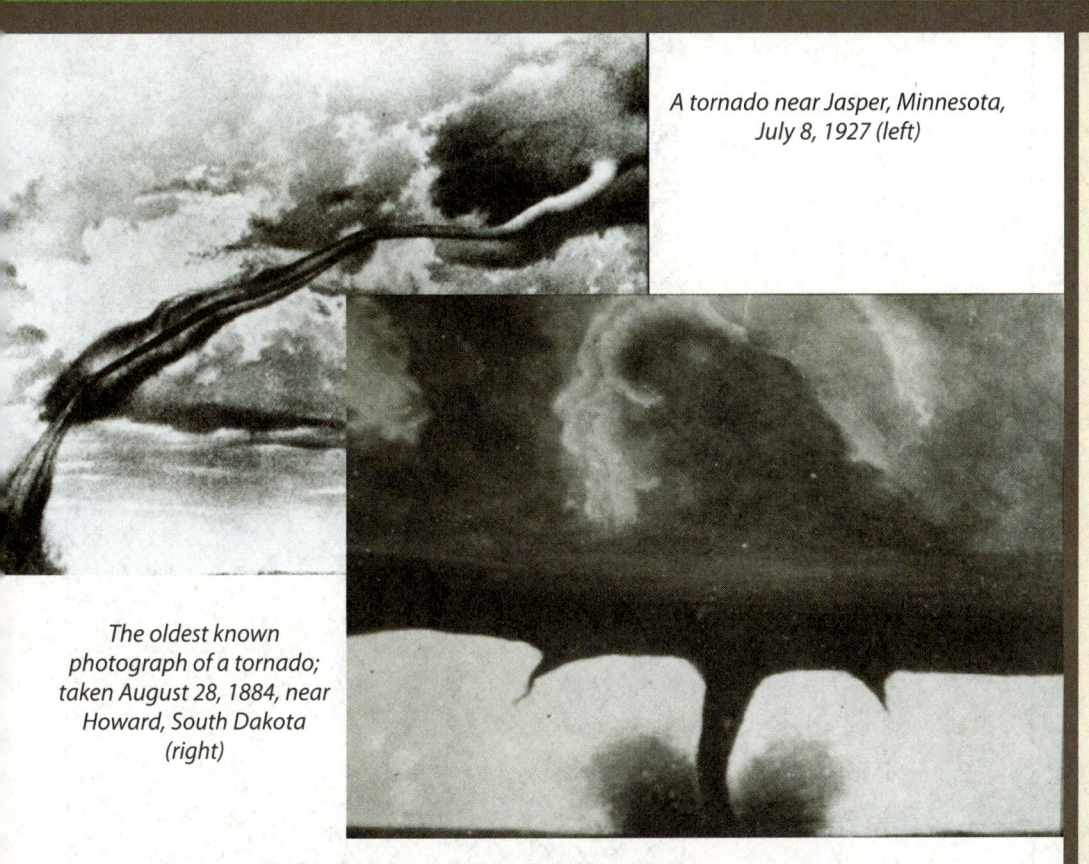

A tornado near Jasper, Minnesota, July 8, 1927 (left)

The oldest known photograph of a tornado; taken August 28, 1884, near Howard, South Dakota (right)

1. America's first tornado scientist was John Park Finley. A tall bear of a man, Finley grew up on a **prosperous** Michigan farm where he learned to keep a close eye on the weather because of its powerful effect on crops. In 1877, Finley enlisted with the U.S. Army Signal Service (later called the Signal Corps), where he received meteorological training and developed a keen interest in tornadoes. A couple of years later, the army sent Finley to study damage caused by a rash of twisters that had swept through the Midwest. Traveling cross-country by horse and buggy, he toured the devastated regions, interviewing eyewitnesses and making meticulous maps showing the twisters' paths. Struck by what he'd witnessed, Finley **embarked** on an exhaustive study of other tornadoes.

Photos: NOAA's National Weather Service (NWS) Collection

prosperous
having or characterized by financial success or good fortune; flourishing; successful

embarked
to set out on

Unlocking the Whirlwind's Mysteries

2. In 1882 he suggested the War Department study an entire tornado season by posting a weather observer in Kansas City, Missouri, who could telegraph reports of severe storms heading across the plains from the East to the West. The plan was approved and Finley served as head of the program. He recruited storm spotters from all over the region to relay weather information straight to his office. With this limited data, Finley began issuing tornado warnings. In 1884 he correctly **predicted** twenty-eight of one hundred tornadoes. These results weren't good enough for the U.S. government, however. Fearing that false alarms caused people to unnecessarily panic, they banned Finley and all meteorologists from using the word tornado in their forecasts. With this ruling, tornado research in the United States ground to a halt until the 1940s.

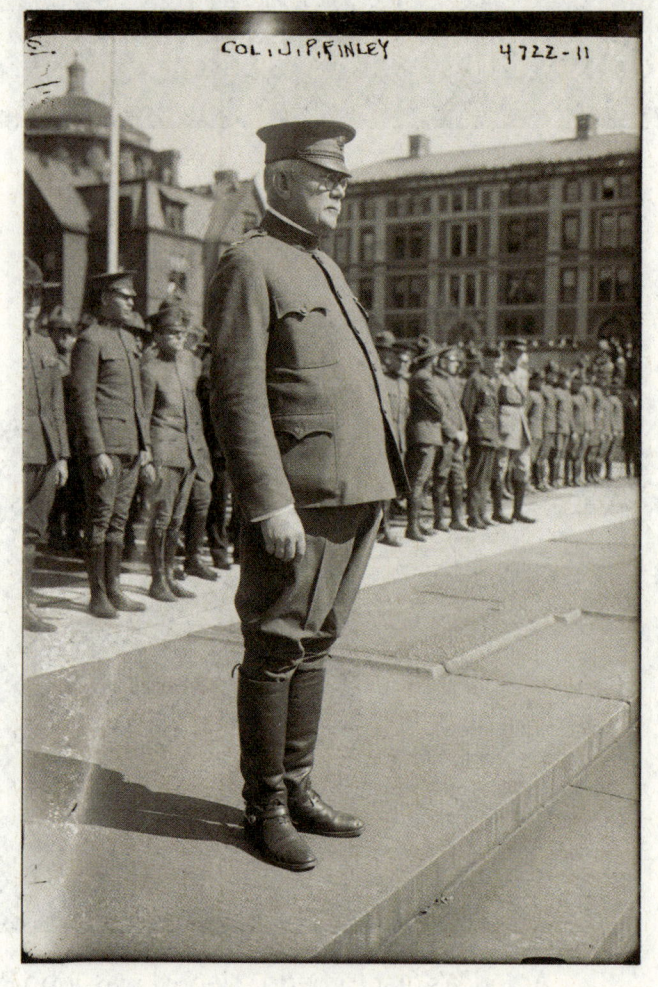

John Park Finley

Photo: Library of Congress, Prints & Photographs Division, LC-DIG-ggbain-27621

Tornado damage at Tinker Air Base, March 20, 1948

Luck Was on Their Side

3   On the morning of March 20, 1948, at Oklahoma City's Tinker Air Base, two air force meteorologists—Captain Robert Miller and his boss Major Ernest J. Fawbush—issued a forecast for gusty winds and possible thunderstorms. Instead, a tornado roared through the base. It rolled big aircraft like they were toys, causing ten million dollars worth of damage and injuring several men in the control tower. The base commander was furious. Couldn't Fawbush and Miller have predicted the tornado? That afternoon the meteorologists started poring through weather charts, analyzing the conditions that existed before every recorded tornado. They noted similarities in the weather patterns.

Photo: Tinker Air Force Base History Office

Unlocking the Whirlwind's Mysteries

4   On March 25, Fawbush and Miller woke up to find these same telltale weather patterns threatening their area. Throughout the morning, conditions deteriorated. The meteorologists debated what to do. Miller estimated that the odds that another tornado would strike the base in a single week were about 20 million to 1. He had visions of what would happen if he told his commander to prepare for a twister and he was wrong again. "I wondered how I would manage as a civilian, perhaps as an elevator operator. It seemed improbable that anyone would employ, as a weather forecaster, an idiot who issued a tornado forecast for a precise location."[1]

5   But finally he and Fawbush decided they couldn't live with themselves if another tornado hit and people got hurt. At 2:50 P.M. they issued a tornado watch. Aircraft were lashed down and stored in hangars. Personnel fled dangerous areas like the control tower. At 3:00 P.M. thunderstorms began to form, and at 6:00 P.M. a tornado hit the base.

6   The Fawbush-Miller tornado forecast was one of the luckiest in history. Even today meteorologists can't say three hours ahead of time that a tornado will strike a particular place on the map. "We're still amazed that they could issue a forecast and have it hit when it did," said meteorologist Steven Weiss.[2]

7   Lucky or not, Fawbush and Miller had identified the basic weather patterns that lead to tornadoes. After that, the air force began to predict twisters using their technique. Sometimes the predictions were right, but sometimes tornadoes formed in areas where they hadn't been expected. It was clear that the Fawbush-Miller method had value but needed to be refined.

8   The air force forecasts were supposed to be kept private, but a few of them leaked out. A 1951 article in the *Saturday Evening Post* said, "A high percentage of [the air force] tornado predictions has been verified. This year, in March and April, the Fawbush-Miller-severe-storm-forecasting technique correctly called the turn on seven twisters—four in Oklahoma, one in Arkansas, and two in Texas."[3] The public began to clamor for access to this information. In 1952 the U.S. Weather Service agreed to start broadcasting tornado warnings.

What's on My Radar Screen?

9   A year later, a tornado passed near Champaign, Illinois, and a radar operator noticed a strange hook shape on his screen. It did not look like anything he'd ever seen before and seemed to be related to the thunderstorm outside. Later analysis showed that the hook had followed the tornado's exact path. Had he accidentally captured the first-ever radar image of a tornado?

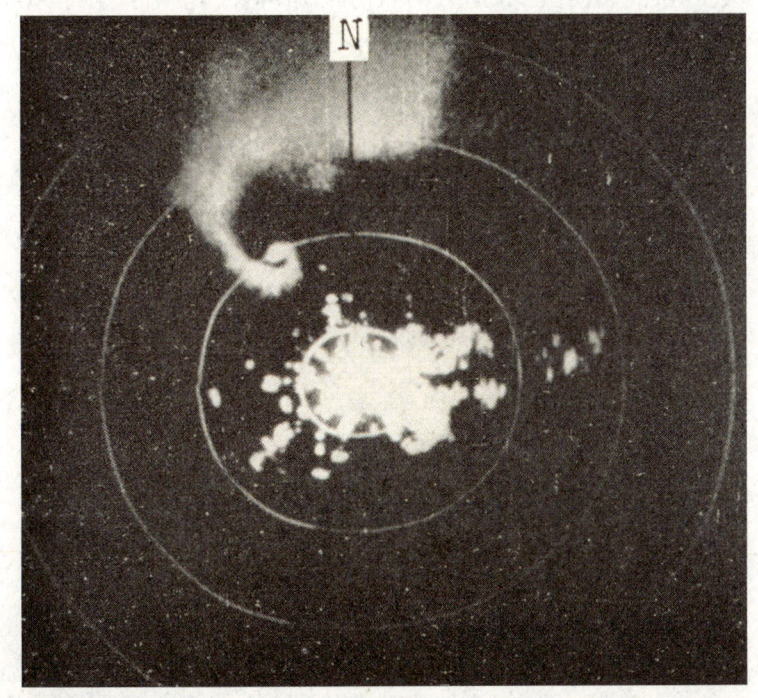

A tornado's hook echo on a radar screen

Photo: NOAA's National Weather Service (NWS) Collection

Unlocking the Whirlwind's Mysteries

10 A brilliant young tornado researcher named Tetsuya Theodore Fujita came to Urbana, Illinois, to try to figure it out. There were only limited data from the storm and yet he kept delving deeper and deeper into the numbers, doing calculations, and, relying on geometry to push his theories forward. He showed that there was actually a wealth of material hidden in the data. "Reading the analysis Fujita made of the Champaign radar findings," said one meteorologist, "is like opening one of those hollow wooden Russian dolls, only to find a dozen more layers of dolls inside."[4]

11 With a **virtuoso's** flourish, Ted Fujita drew complicated maps of the tornado and its storm. He proved that the hook was not the tornado itself, but belonged to a rotation up in the thunderclouds. He said this rotation resembled "a miniature hurricane in many respects."[5] He named the mini-hurricane the "mesocyclone." Fujita's discovery of the mesocyclone's radar signature meant that forecasters had a valuable new tool for identifying potential tornadic storms. Soon, the government decided to install radar towers across Tornado Alley to watch for Fujita's mesocyclones.

> **virtuoso**
> a person who is extremely skilled at something, especially at playing an instrument or performing

---

1. "1948 Prediction Spurs Tornado Forecasting," [Online] Available at http://www.usatoday.com/weather/tornado/w1stfcst.htm, March 14, 2000.
2. "1948 Prediction Spurs Tornado Forecasting."
3. "1948 Prediction Spurs Tornado Forecasting."
4. Jeff Rosenfeld, "Mr. Tornado: the Life and Career of Ted Fujita," *Weatherwise*, May–June 1999, pp. 21–22.
5. Keay Davidson, *Twister: The Science of Tornadoes and the Making of an Adventure Movie* (New York: Pocket Books, 1996) p. 78.

Reading Passage 2 for Lessons 7–8

Tornado Scales

Tornado observed by the VORTEX-99 team on May 3, 1999, in central Oklahoma. Note the tube-like condensation funnel, attached to the rotating cloud base, surrounded by a translucent dust cloud.

1. Before 1971, there was no way for scientists to rank tornadoes by their strength. How big the tornado looked had no bearing on how strong it actually was. In 1971, Professor Fujita came up with a system to rank tornadoes according to how much damage they cause. This was called the Fujita Scale. As of February 1, 2007, a new scale for rating the strength of tornadoes is being used. It is called the **Enhanced** Fujita Scale.

2. The Enhanced Fujita Scale or EF Scale has six categories from zero to five, with EF5 being the highest degree of damage. The Scale was used the first time as three separate tornadoes took place in central Florida early on February 2, 2007. These tornadoes destroyed many houses and businesses and killed at least 21 people. And these tornadoes were only rated EF3 tornadoes!

Photo: OAR/ERL/National Severe Storms Laboratory (NSSL), courtesy of NOAA

Tornado Scales

3. Scientists have to figure out how strong a tornado is after it hits. Because the scale is based on the damage caused by it, they can't predict how strong a tornado would be before it happens.

Original Fujita Scale		Enhanced Fujita Scale	
F5	261–318 mph	EF5	+200 mph
F4	207–260 mph	EF4	166–200 mph
F3	158–206 mph	EF3	136–165 mph
F2	113–157 mph	EF2	111–135 mph
F1	73–112 mph	EF1	86–110 mph
F0	<73 mph	EF0	65–85 mph

amended
changed for the better; improved

4. The Fujita Scale has been improved and **amended** in a way that affects the original estimated wind speeds. In addition, to cover the many variables in building materials, there are now 28 categories of construction by which to measure a tornado's destructive power.

Enhanced Scale Includes Detailed Damage Categories/Descriptions

- Small barns, farm outbuildings
- One- or two-family residences
- Single-wide mobile home
- Double-wide mobile home
- Apt, condo, townhouse (3 stories or less)
- Motel Masonry apt. or motel
- Small retail bldg. (fast food)
- Small professional (doctor office, branch bank)
- Strip mall
- Large shopping mall
- Large, isolated ("big box") retail bldg.
- Automobile showroom
- Automotive service building
- School—1-story elementary (interior or exterior halls)
- School—jr. or sr. high school
- Low-rise (1–4 story) bldg.
- Mid-rise (5–20 story) bldg.
- High-rise (over 20 stories)
- Institutional bldg. (hospital, govt. or university)
- Metal building system
- Service station canopy
- Warehouse (tilt-up walls or heavy timber)
- Transmission line tower
- Free standing tower
- Free standing pole (light, flag, luminary)
- Tree—hardwood
- Tree—softwood

Photo: OAR/ERL/National Severe Storms Laboratory (NSSL)

Lessons 7–8

The Original Fujita Scale

F-Scale Number	Intensity Phrase	Wind Speed	Type of Damage Done
F0	Gale tornado	40–72 mph	Some damage to chimneys; breaks branches off trees; pushes over shallow-rooted trees; damages sign boards.
F1	Moderate tornado	73–112 mph	The lower limit is the beginning of hurricane wind speed; peels surface off roofs; mobile homes pushed off foundations or overturned; moving autos pushed off the roads; attached garages may be destroyed.
F2	Significant tornado	113–157 mph	Considerable damage. Roofs torn off frame houses; mobile homes demolished; boxcars pushed over; large trees snapped or uprooted; light object missiles generated.
F3	Severe tornado	158–206 mph	Roof and some walls torn off well-constructed houses; trains overturned; most trees in forest uprooted.
F4	Devastating tornado	207–260 mph	Well-constructed houses leveled; structures with weak foundations blown off some distance; cars thrown and large missiles generated.
F5	Incredible tornado	261–318 mph	Strong frame houses lifted off foundations and carried considerable distances to disintegrate; automobile sized missiles fly through the air in excess of 100 meters; trees debarked; steel reinforced concrete structures badly damaged.
F6	Inconceivable tornado	319–379 mph	These winds are very unlikely. The small area of damage they might produce would probably not be recognizable along with the mess produced by F4 and F5 wind that would surround the F6 winds. Missiles, such as cars and refrigerators would do serious secondary damage that could not be directly identified as F6 damage. If this level is ever achieved, evidence for it might only be found in some manner of ground swirl pattern, for it may never be identifiable through engineering studies.

Whirlwind's Timeline

1877 — Finley enlists in Army Signal Service (later called Signal Corps), begins to study tornadoes

Fujita Scales

1. What is the author's purpose for paragraph ____?

   _____
   _____
   _____

2. Look at the Original and Enhanced Fujita Scales.

   a. What is different between these two scales?

   _____
   _____

   b. What is the same about these two scales?

   _____
   _____

3. What is the author's purpose for including the information in the Enhanced Scale Includes Detailed Damage Categories/Descriptions chart?

   _____
   _____

4. Review the Original Fujita Scale matrix.

   a. What wind speed will lift a strong frame house off of its foundation?

   _____

   b. What is the F-Scale Number of a significant tornado?

   _____

   c. What is the Intensity Phrase of a tornado that has wind speeds between 207–260 mph?

   _____

LESSON 8 · FOUNDATIONS · EXTREME WEATHER—LEVEL D · 47

Witnessing a Tornado

Write a paragraph describing what you would witness if you walked into a city that was hit by an F4 tornado. According to what you have read, what are things that you would see, feel, and smell.

Reading Passage for Lesson 9

Recent Natural Disasters

Aerial photo of St. John's Hospital in Joplin, Mo. after a deadly tornado hit the city.

Preliminary Tornado Statistics Including Records Set in 2011

1. On Sunday, May 22, 2011, an EF-5 tornado hit the city of Joplin, Mo., leaving an estimated 132 people dead and 750 others injured, with 156 unaccounted for in Joplin.

2. The Joplin tornado is the deadliest since modern recordkeeping began in 1950 and is ranked 8th among the deadliest tornadoes in U.S. history.

3. The deadliest tornado on record in the U.S. was on March 18, 1925. The "Tri-State Tornado" (MO, IL, IN) had a 291-mile path, was rated F5 based on a historical assessment, and caused 695 **fatalities**. The EF-5 Joplin tornado had winds in excess of 200 mph, was ¾ of a mile wide, and six miles long.

Photo: NOAA

preliminary
introductory; preparatory

fatalities
deaths from an accident or disaster

Recent Natural Disasters

Smoke from Southern California wildfires drift over the Pacific Ocean

Wildfires in the West

4   In what seemed like the blink of an eye, wildfires ignited in the paper-dry, drought-stricken vegetation of Southern California over the weekend of October 20, 2007, and exploded into massive infernos that forced hundreds of thousands of people to evacuate their communities. Driven by Santa Ana winds, fires grew thousands of acres in just one to two days. The fires sped down from the mountains into the outskirts of coastal cities, including San Diego.

5   The 2007 fire season included 23 wildfires in an area of seven counties. More than two thousand homes were destroyed and seven people died.

Photo: NASA

Lesson 9

After a Flood of Record on the Mississippi, Flooding Veers North and West

6 After weeks of responding to the historic flooding along the Mississippi River, U.S. Geological Survey scientists have shifted some focus to the West. Many communities in South Dakota, North Dakota, Montana, Colorado, Wyoming and Iowa are dealing with record floodwaters and bracing for more flooding in the upcoming weeks.

7 This latest round of flooding is due to extreme spring **precipitation**, which could be **compounded** by snowmelt in the mountains in the near future. Though the Missouri River flows into the Mississippi River, flooding on the Missouri River is not expected to significantly affect current flooding on the Mississippi River.

> **compounded**
> to have made something worse by increasing or adding to it

Release of water from a reservoir along the Missouri River in South Dakota

8 USGS measurements are the **cornerstone** of National Weather Service predictions and forecasts. When flooding happens, USGS field crews are among the first to respond. During and after storms and floods, USGS field crews measure the streamflow and height of rivers. Crews repair and install **streamgages** to ensure the accurate and reliable data continues to make it to USGS partners like the National Weather Service and Army Corps of Engineers, as well as the public, emergency managers and communities.

> **cornerstone**
> something that is essential, indispensable, or basic

Photo: Joyce Williamson, USGS

FOUNDATIONS • EXTREME WEATHER—LEVEL D | **51**

Recent Natural Disasters

9   The 2006 image (left) shows the Mississippi river in a more normal state, while the 2011 image (right) shows the massive flooding. The dark blue tones represent water or flooded areas, the light green is cleared fields, and light tones are clouds. This recent Landsat satellite data captured by the U.S. Geological Survey and NASA on May 10, 2011 show the major flooding of the Mississippi River along the state borders of Tennessee, Kentucky, Missouri, and Arkansas as seen from 438 miles above the Earth.

Images: USGS/NASA

Recent Natural Disasters Chart

Tornado	Wildfires	Flooding

Three Disasters

Think about the three disasters you read about today. Which of these events could happen in your area? Which do you think could cause the most damage? Why do you think this?

Reading Passage 1 for Lesson 10

Wild Weather

1. At any time, across the world, about 2,000 thunderstorms are lighting up the sky with giant electrical sparks. A bolt of lightning can reach 54,000 degrees F (30,000°C), five times hotter than the surface of the Sun. The massive electrical charge a lightning bolt carries can kill in an instant. Most thunderstorms happen in summer, when warm air rises to form thunderclouds. These storms can bring torrential rain or stinging hail. Meteorologists track the path of thunderstorms using information from satellites, weather stations on the ground, and specially adapted weather planes that can fly into storms.

Photo: C. Clark, NOAA Photo Library, NOAA Central Library; OAR/ERL/National Severe Storms Laboratory (NSSL)

Wild Weather

conductor
a substance, body, or system that transmits electricity, heat

2   This dramatic photograph shows lightning striking the Eiffel Tower in Paris, France. Like other tall buildings, the Eiffel Tower is protected from damage from lightning strikes by a lightning **conductor**—a metal cable or strap that leads the electrical charge down to the ground where it discharges harmlessly.

Lightning striking the Eiffel Tower, June 3, 1902, at 9:20 P.M. The photo, taken by M. G. Loppé, is one of the earliest photographs of lightning in an urban setting.

How Rainclouds Form

3   The Sun's heat makes water from the oceans and on land evaporate into the air. The moist, warm air rises and becomes cooler. As it cools, the water vapor in it condenses to form clouds. The water droplets in the cloud link together and grow heavier. When the cloud is thick enough, the water falls back to Earth as rain, hail, or snow. Factors that make warm, moist air rise rapidly, creating storm clouds, occur where one air mass overrides another (frontal wedging), where air converges, and where mountains uplift moving air.

Photo: NOAA's National Weather Service (NWS) Collection

Lesson 10

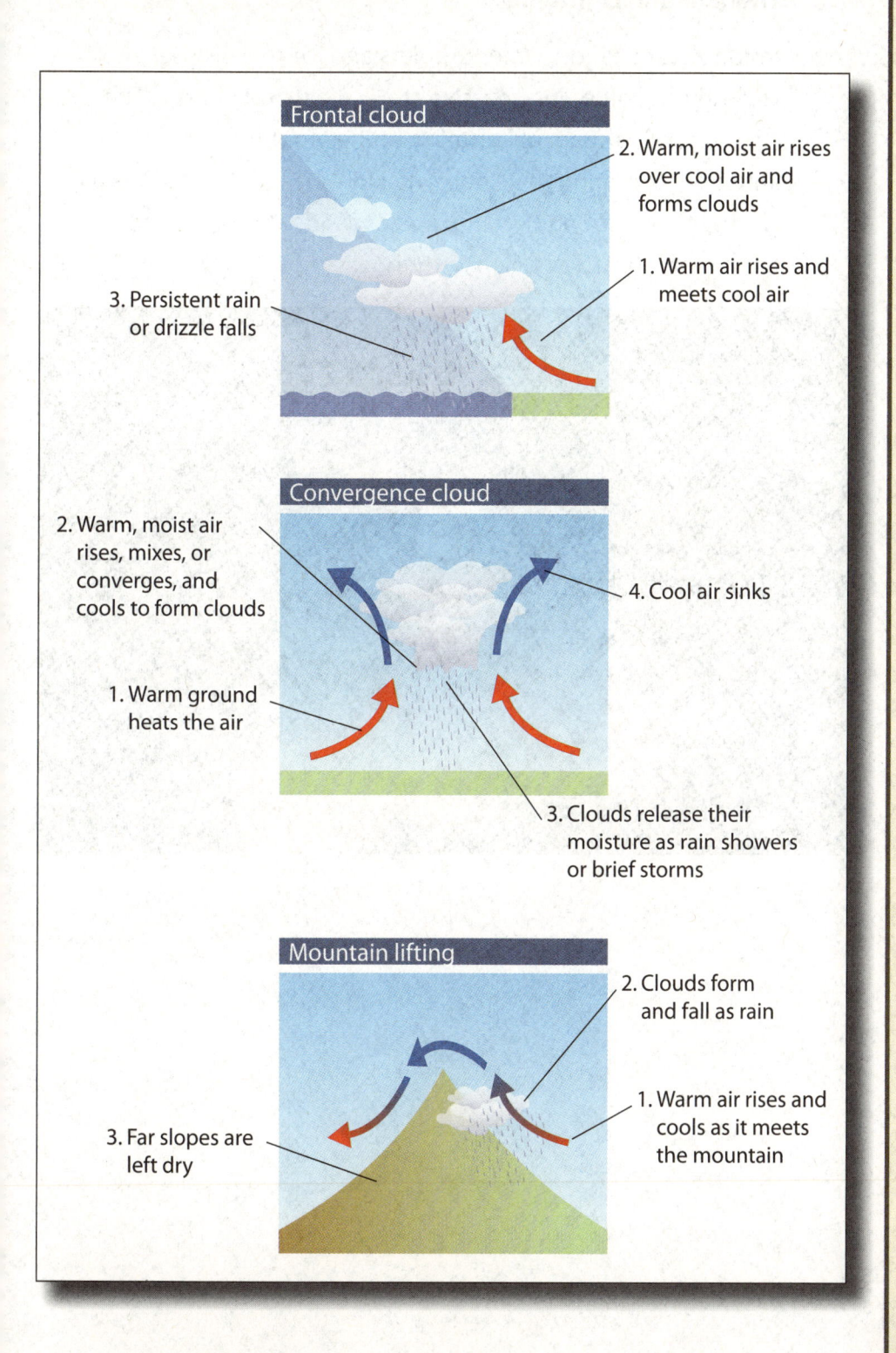

Frontal cloud

1. Warm air rises and meets cool air
2. Warm, moist air rises over cool air and forms clouds
3. Persistent rain or drizzle falls

Convergence cloud

1. Warm ground heats the air
2. Warm, moist air rises, mixes, or converges, and cools to form clouds
3. Clouds release their moisture as rain showers or brief storms
4. Cool air sinks

Mountain lifting

1. Warm air rises and cools as it meets the mountain
2. Clouds form and fall as rain
3. Far slopes are left dry

Art: Copyright © Pearson Education, Inc., or its affiliates.

FOUNDATIONS • EXTREME WEATHER—LEVEL D

Wild Weather

Thunder and Lightning

4   Inside a storm cloud, water droplets and ice crystals rise and fall violently, building up a massive **static electrical charge**. The charge sends a spark of lightning to the ground, creating fork lightning, or among the clouds, making sheet lightning. The air around the lightning heats up and expands, creating a shock wave that is heard as a clap of thunder.

Photo: NOAA Photo Library, NOAA Central Library; OAR/ERL/National Severe Storms Laboratory (NSSL)

Thunderstorm Basics

What is a thunderstorm?

1. A thunderstorm is a rain shower during which you hear thunder. Since thunder comes from lightning, all thunderstorms have lightning. A thunderstorm is classified as "severe" when it contains one or more of the following: hail three-quarter inch or greater, winds gusting in excess of 50 knots (57.5 mph), tornado.

What is known?

2. An average thunderstorm is 15 miles in diameter and lasts an average of 30 minutes. At any given moment, there are roughly 2,000 thunderstorms in progress around the world. It is estimated that there are 100,000 thunderstorms each year. About 10% of these reach severe levels.

Photo: VORTEX II/Sean Waugh NOAA/NSSL

Thunderstorm Basics

How does a thunderstorm form?

3. Three basic ingredients are required for a thunderstorm to form: moisture, rising unstable air (air that keeps rising when given a nudge), and a lifting mechanism to provide the "nudge."

4. The sun heats the surface of the earth, which warms the air above it. If this warm surface air is forced to rise—hills or mountains, or areas where warm/cold or wet/dry air bump together can cause rising motion—it will continue to rise as long as it weighs less and stays warmer than the air around it.

5. As the air rises, it transfers heat from the surface of the earth to the upper levels of the atmosphere (the process of convection). The water vapor it contains begins to cool, releasing the heat, and it condenses into a cloud. The cloud eventually grows upward into areas where the temperature is below freezing.

Photo: NOAA Photo Library, NOAA Central Library; OAR/ERL/National Severe Storms Laboratory (NSSL)

6 Some of the water vapor turns to ice and some of it turns into water droplets. Both have electrical charges. Ice particles usually have positive charges, and rain droplets usually have negative charges. When the charges build up enough, they are discharged in a bolt of lightning, which causes the sound waves we hear as thunder.

The Thunderstorm Life Cycle

7 Thunderstorms have a life cycle of three stages: The developing stage, the **mature** stage, and the **dissipating** stage.

8 The *developing stage* of a thunderstorm is marked by a cumulus cloud that is being pushed upward by a rising column of air (updraft). The cumulus cloud soon looks like a tower (called towering cumulus) as the updraft continues to develop. There is little to no rain during this stage but occasional lightning. The developing stage lasts about 10 minutes.

9 The thunderstorm enters the *mature stage* when the updraft continues to feed the storm, but precipitation begins to fall out of the storm, and a downdraft begins (a column of air pushing downward). When the downdraft and rain-cooled air spreads out

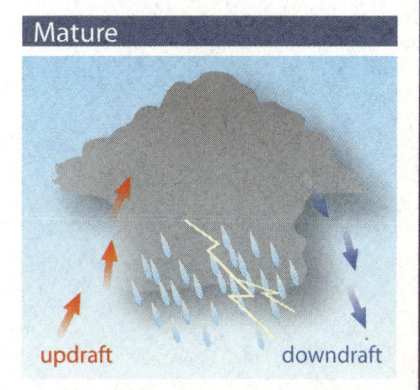

> **dissipating**
> scattering in various directions; dispersing; dispelling

Art: Copyright © Pearson Education, Inc., or its affiliates.

Thunderstorm Basics

along the ground it forms a gust front, or a line of gusty winds. The mature stage is the most likely time for hail, heavy rain, frequent lightning, strong winds, and tornadoes. The storm occasionally has a black or dark green appearance.

10 Eventually, a large amount of precipitation is produced and the updraft is overcome by the downdraft beginning the *dissipating stage*. At the ground, the gust front moves out a long distance from the storm and cuts off the warm moist air that was feeding the thunderstorm. Rainfall decreases in intensity, but lightning remains a danger.

About Thunderstorms Chart

Known about Thunderstorms	Learned about Thunderstorms

How Rainclouds Form Graphic Organizer

Stages of a Thunderstorm Chart

Complete the chart showing the stages of a thunderstorm.

Developing Stage	Mature Stage	Dissipating Stage

Storm News Report

You are a newscaster reporting on a coming storm. Write what you would say to the audience about what to expect from the storm.

Reading Passage for Lessons 11–12

Hurricanes
The Greatest Storms on Earth

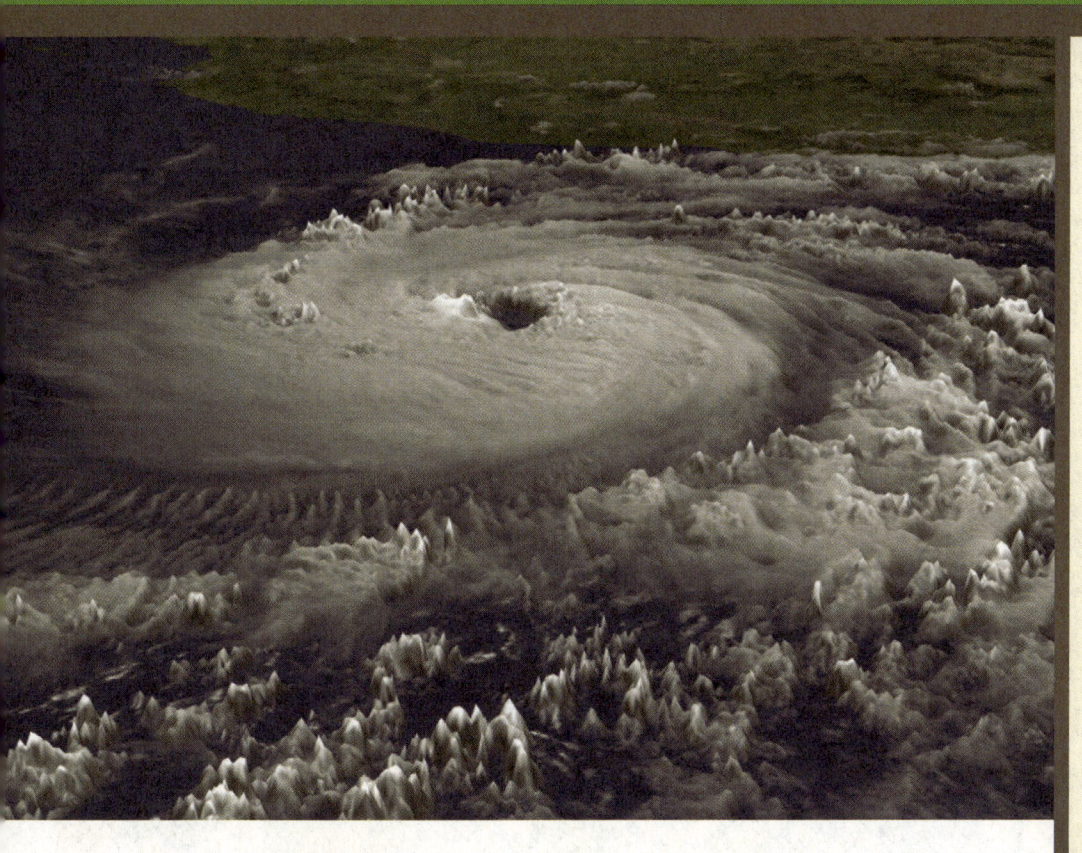

Photo: NOAA

Hurricane Anatomy

1. During hurricane development, certain characteristics become more prominent as the storm strengthens. At the center of the hurricane is the eye, a cloud-free area of sinking air and light winds that is usually from 10 to 65 kilometers in diameter. As air rises in the thunderstorms surrounding the eye, some of it is forced towards the center, where it **converges** and sinks. As this air sinks, it compresses and warms to create an environment (mostly) free of clouds and precipitation. The eye is the calmest part of the storm because the strong surface winds converging towards the center never actually reach the exact center of the storm, but instead form a cylinder of relatively calm air.

converges
moves toward the same point and comes closer together

FOUNDATIONS • EXTREME WEATHER—LEVEL D | 67

Hurricanes

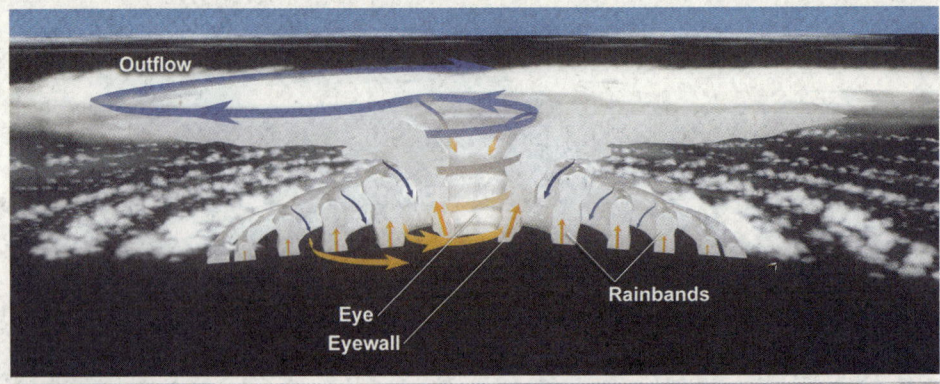

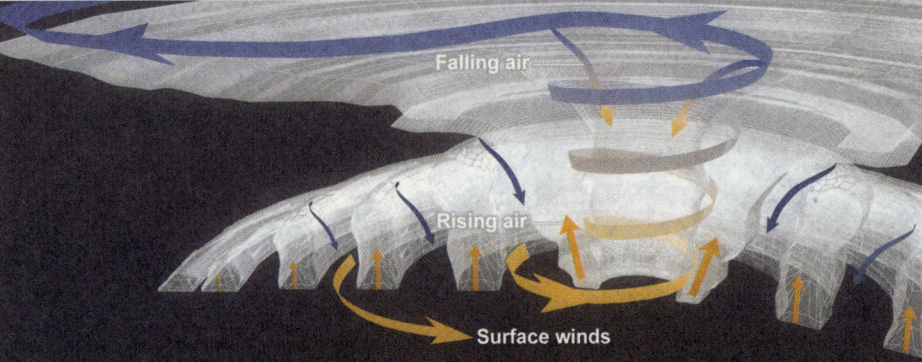

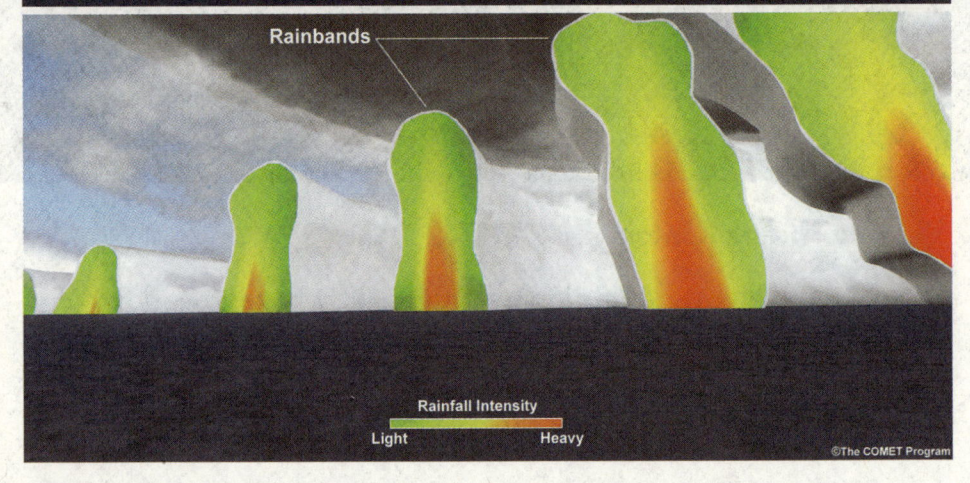

concentric
having a common center, as circles or spheres

(Top) Surrounding the eye of the hurricane is a ring of thunderstorms, called the eyewall. Rainbands surround the eye of the storm in **concentric** circles. In the eyewall and in the rainbands, warm, moist air rises, while in the eye and around the rainbands, air from higher in the atmosphere sinks back toward the surface. The rising air cools, and water vapor in the air condenses into rain. Sinking air warms and dries, creating a calm, cloud-free area in the eye.

(Middle) Low pressure at the ocean surface in the heart of the hurricane draws in surrounding air. These spiraling winds pick up speed as they approach the eye, pulling more heat and moisture from the ocean surface.

(Bottom). The stronger the convection in the thunderstorms becomes, the more rain they produce. The more rain they produce, the more heat they release into the surrounding atmosphere, further fueling the storm.

Graphics Copyright © National Center for Atmospheric Research/The COMET Program

2. Bordering the eye of a mature hurricane is the eye wall, a ring of tall thunderstorms that produce heavy rains and very strong winds. The most destructive section of the storm is in the eye wall on the side where the wind blows in the same direction as the storm's forward motion. For example, in a hurricane that is moving due west, the most intense winds would be found on the northern side of the storm, since the hurricane's winds are added to the storm's forward motion.

3. Surrounding the eye wall are curved bands of clouds that trail away in a spiral fashion, suitably called spiraling rain bands. The rain bands are capable of producing heavy bursts of rain and wind, perhaps one-half or two-thirds the strength of those associated with the eye wall.

Storm Surge

4. As a hurricane moves closer to land, coastal communities begin to feel the effects of heavy rain, strong winds, and tornadoes. However, its most destructive weapon is the accompanying storm surge, a rise in the ocean levels of up to 10 meters (about 33 feet). When a hurricane approaches the coast, an 80-to-160-kilometer-wide dome of ocean water sweeps over the coastline. Storm surges have demolished marinas, piers, boardwalks, houses, and other shoreline structures, while eroding beaches and washing out coastal roads and railroads. Strong onshore winds pushing the ocean surface ahead of the storm on the right side of the storm track (left side in the Southern Hemisphere) is the primary cause of the storm surge. This wall of water is greatest when the arrival of the storm coincides with the occurrence of an astronomical high tide.

Hurricanes

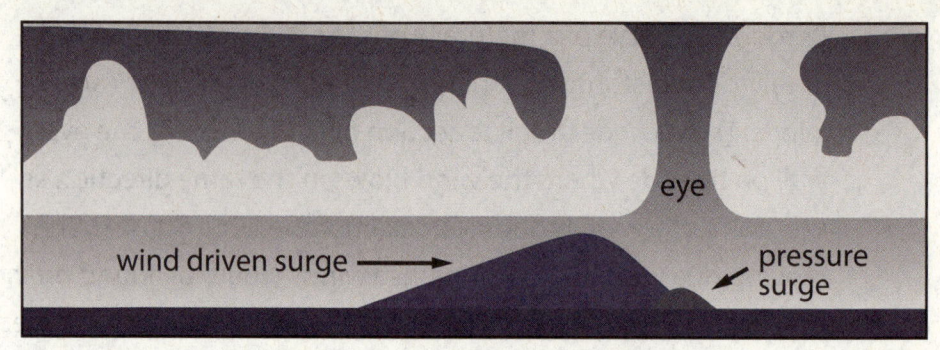

Strong winds are responsible for most of a hurricane's storm surge, but the extremely low air pressure in the eye of the storm also plays a small role. The low pressure in the eye allows the surrounding atmosphere to compress the ocean surface into a small bulge.

The Saffir-Simpson Scale

5 In the early 1970s, a classification system was designed to quantify the level of damage and flooding expected from a hurricane. This system was conceived by Herbert Saffir, a consulting engineer, and Robert Simpson, then the director of the National Hurricane Center. Using a mix of structural engineering and **meteorology**, they constructed the Saffir-Simpson Hurricane Intensity Scale, or simply, the Saffir-Simpson Scale. Consisting of 5 categories (1 being the weakest and 5 being the strongest), the scale corresponds to a hurricane's central pressure, maximum sustained winds, and storm surge. Sustained wind speeds are the determining factor in the scale, as storm surge values are highly dependent on the slope of the continental shelf in the landfall region. Categories 3, 4, and 5 are considered major (intense) hurricanes, capable of inflicting great damage and loss of life.

6 **Category 1:** Winds 119–153 km/hr (74–95 mph). Storm surge generally 4–5 feet above normal. No real damage to building structures. Damage primarily to unanchored mobile homes, shrubbery, and trees. Some damage to poorly constructed signs. Also, some coastal road flooding and minor pier damage.

Art: Copyright © Pearson Education, Inc., or its affiliates, based on work by Robert Simmon, NASA GSFC.

High seas and winds from Hurricane Dennis flooded this coastal road in North Carolina (left). Winds from Hurricane Wilma shattered windows in Miami, Florida, in 2005 (right).

7 **Category 2:** Winds 154–177 km/hr (96–110 mph). Storm surge generally 6–8 feet above normal. Some roofing material, door, and window damage of buildings. Considerable damage to shrubbery and trees, with some trees blown down. Considerable damage to mobile homes, poorly constructed signs, and piers. Coastal and low-lying escape routes flood 2–4 hours before arrival of the hurricane center. Small craft in unprotected anchorages break moorings.

8 **Category 3:** Winds 178–209 km/hr (111–130 mph). Storm surge generally 9–12 ft above normal. Some structural damage to small residences and utility buildings, with a minor amount of curtain wall (non-load-bearing exterior wall) failures. Damage to shrubbery and trees, with foliage blown off trees, and large trees blown down. Mobile homes and poorly constructed signs are destroyed. Low-lying escape routes are cut by rising water 3–5 hours before arrival of the center of the hurricane. Flooding near the coast destroys smaller structures, with larger structures damaged by battering from floating debris. This photo shows extensive damage to private homes and boats in Christian Pass, Mississippi, in the aftermath of Hurricane Katrina.

Photos: Dave Gatley/FEMA (top left); © iStockphoto.com/Federico Montemurro (top right); Andrea Booher/FEMA (bottom)

Hurricanes

9. **Category 4:** Winds 210–249 km/hr (131–155 mph). Storm surge generally 13–18 feet above normal. More extensive curtain wall failures, with some complete roof structure failures on small residences. Shrubs, trees, and all signs are blown down. Complete destruction of mobile homes. Extensive damage to doors and windows. Low-lying escape routes may be cut by rising water 3–5 hours before arrival of the center of the hurricane. Major damage to lower floors of structures near the shore. Terrain lower than 10 feet above sea level may be flooded. Hurricane winds completely toppled this house in North Carolina.

10. **Category 5:** Winds greater than 249 km/hr (155 mph). Storm surge generally greater than 18 feet above normal. Complete roof failure on many residences and industrial buildings. Some complete building failures, with small utility buildings blown over or away. All shrubs, trees, and signs blown down. Complete destruction of mobile homes. Severe and extensive window and door damage. Low-lying escape routes are cut by rising water 3–5 hours before arrival of the center of the hurricane. Major damage to lower floors of all structures located less than 15 feet above sea level and within 500 yards of the shoreline. This photo shows the aftermath of Hurricane Andrew in 1992.

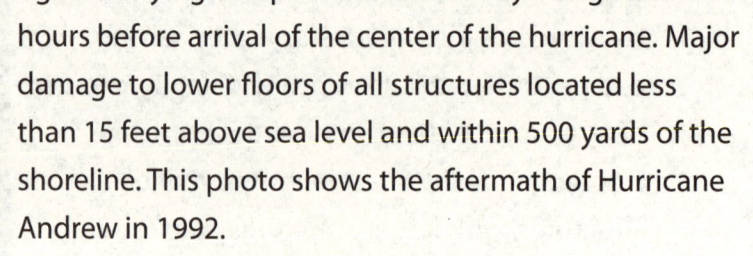

Photos: Dave Gatley/FEMA News Photo (top); NOAA's National Weather Service (NWS) Collection (bottom)

Saffir-Simpson Hurricane Scale

Category	Winds	Effects
1	74–95 mph	No real damage to building structures. Damage primarily to unanchored mobile homes, shrubbery, and trees. Also, some coastal road flooding and minor pier damage.
2	96–110 mph	Some roofing material, door, and window damage to buildings. Considerable damage to vegetation, mobile homes, and piers. Coastal and low-lying escape routes flood 2–4 hours before arrival of center. Small craft in unprotected anchorages break moorings.
3	111–130 mph	Some structural damage to small residences and utility buildings with a minor amount of curtainwall failures. Mobile homes are destroyed. Flooding near the coast destroys smaller structures with larger structures damaged by floating debris. Terrain continuously lower than 5 feet ASL may be flooded inland 8 miles or more.
4	131–155 mph	More extensive curtainwall failures with some complete roof structure failure on small residences. Major erosion of beach. Major damage to lower floors of structures near the shore. Terrain continuously lower than 10 feet ASL may be flooded requiring massive evacuation of residential areas inland as far as 6 miles.
5	greater than 155 mph	Complete roof failure on many residences and industrial buildings. Some complete building failures with small utility buildings blown over or away. Major damage to lower floors of all structures located less than 15 feet ASL and within 500 yards of the shoreline. Massive evacuation of residential areas on low ground within 5 to 10 miles of the shoreline may be required.

About Hurricanes Chart

Known about Hurricanes	Learned about Hurricanes

Hurricane Illustration

Draw a picture to illustrate the information in paragraph 2.

Hurricane If/Then Statements

Part 1

Write an if/then statement about what you read today (paragraphs 1–3).

Part 2

1. If you are in the northern side of the storm pass, then _____.

2. If a hurricane moves closer to land, then _____.

3. If _____, then the storm surge is caused.

4. If there is considerable damage to mobile homes, poorly constructed signs, and piers, then it is a category _____.

5. If the wind speeds are below 74 mph, then _____.

Part 3

Write an if/then statement about extreme weather.

Reading Passage for Lesson 13

Hurricane Hazards

Storm surge destruction from Hurricane Katrina along the coastline of Gulfport, Mississippi

One of the most dramatic, damaging, and potentially deadly events that occur in this country is a hurricane.

1. Hurricanes are products of the tropical ocean and atmosphere. Powered by heat from the sea, they are steered **erratically** by the easterly trade winds and the temperate westerly winds, as well as by their own energy. As they move ashore, they bring with them a storm surge of ocean water along the coastline, high winds, tornadoes, torrential rains, and flooding.

Photo: Lieut. Commander Mark Moran, NOAA Corps, NMAO/AOC

erratically
having no certain or definite course; wandering; not fixed

Hurricane Hazards

Hurricane Irene struck the United States coastline in August of 2011.

2   Each year on average, ten tropical storms develop over the Atlantic Ocean, Caribbean Sea, or Gulf of Mexico. About six of these typically strengthen enough to become hurricanes. Many of these remain over the ocean with little or no impact on the continental United States. However, about five hurricanes strike the United States coastline every three years. Of these five, two will be major hurricanes measuring a category 3 or higher (defined as having winds above 111 miles per hour) on the Saffir-Simpson Scale. These storms can end up costing our nation millions, if not billions, of dollars in damages.

3   During a hurricane, homes, businesses, public buildings, and **infrastructure** may be damaged or destroyed by many different storm hazards. Debris can break windows and doors, allowing high winds and rain inside the home. In extreme storms (such as Hurricanes Hugo, Andrew and Katrina), the force of the wind alone can cause tremendous devastation, as trees and power lines

> **infrastructure**
> *the fundamental facilities and systems serving a country, city, or area, such as transportation and communication systems, power plants, and schools*

Photo: NASA

topple and weak elements of homes and buildings fail. Roads and bridges can be washed away and homes saturated by flooding. Destructive tornadoes can also be present well away from the storms center during landfall. Yet, storm surge alone poses the highest threat to life and destruction in many coastal areas throughout the United States and territories. And these threats are not limited to the coastline—they can extend hundreds of miles inland, under the right conditions.

Storm Surge

The greatest potential for loss of life related to a hurricane is from the storm surge!

4   Storm surge is simply water that is pushed toward the shore by the force of the winds swirling around the storm. This advancing surge combines with the normal **tides** to create the hurricane storm tide, which can increase the mean water level to heights impacting roads, homes and other critical infrastructure. In addition, wind driven waves are superimposed on the storm tide. This rise in water level can cause severe flooding in coastal areas, particularly when the storm tide coincides with the normal high tides. Because much of the United States' densely populated Atlantic and Gulf Coast coastlines lie less than 10 feet above mean sea level, the danger from storm tides is tremendous.

Sixteen feet of storm surge struck the Florida Panhandle during Hurricane Eloise, September, 1975.

Photo: NOAA's National Weather Service (NWS) Collection

Hurricane Hazards

Utility poles and lines down in Garden City, South Carolina after passage of Hurricane Hugo

5   The storm surge combined with wave action can cause extensive damage, severely erode beaches and coastal highways. With major storms like Katrina, Camille, and Hugo, complete devastation of coastal communities occurred. Many buildings withstand hurricane force winds until their foundations, undermined by erosion, are weakened and fail.

Inland Flooding from Hurricanes

The next time you hear hurricane—think inland flooding!

6   While storm surge has the highest potential to cause hurricane related deaths, more people died from inland flooding associated with tropical systems from 1970 to 1999. Since the 1970's, inland flooding has been responsible for more than half of all deaths associated with tropical cyclones in the United States. Flooding from hurricanes can occur hundreds of miles from the coast placing communities, which would not normally be affected by the strongest hurricane winds, in great danger.

Photo: Wes Tyler, South Carolina Climatological Office

Lesson 13

Facts about Inland Flooding from Hurricanes

- From 1970 to 1999, 78% of children killed by tropical cyclones drowned in freshwater floods.
- One cubic yard of water weighs 1700 lbs. The average automobile weighs 3400 lbs. Many automobiles will float in just 2 feet of water.
- The average person can be swept off their feet in 6 inches of moving water.
- The average automobile can be swept off the road in 12 inches of moving water.
- At least 23% of U.S. tropical cyclone deaths occur to people who drown in, or attempting to abandon, their cars.
- Rainfall is typically heavier with slower moving storms.
- Some of the greatest rainfall amounts associated with tropical systems occur from weaker Tropical Storms that have a slow forward speed (1 to 10 mph) or stall over an area. Due to the amount of rainfall a Tropical Storm can produce, they are capable of causing as much damage as a category 2 hurricane.

Flooding in Ashville, North Carolina, caused by Hurricane Francis in 2004

Photo: FEMA/Leif Skoogfors

Storm Surge Web

storm surge

Reading Passage for Lesson 14

Can Anyone Stop the Waves?

The Thames River Barrier in operation with its flood gates closed

1. During a hurricane, giant waves crash against a sea wall. The tons of earth and stone in this artificial barrier usually hold back a storm because the wall has been designed tall enough and strong enough to withstand huge waves. Recently, however, **engineers** around the world have begun to think "outside the wall." They have developed radical new designs for holding back the water's fury.

2. For example, instead of standing tall, London's Thames River Barrier—a sea wall that moves—is usually lying on the river floor. But it wasn't knocked down by a storm. Designed in the early 1980's, its semicircular gates are arranged to pivot downward when not in use. This lets ships pass freely across, something that would be impossible with a rigid sea wall. However, let a storm threaten, and **hydraulic** rams raise the wall's ten interlocking sections into place, forming a wave-tight steel barrier that is five stories high and one-third of a mile across.

hydraulic
operated by, moved by, or employing water or other liquids in motion

Photo: © iStockphoto.com/Anthony Baggett

Can Anyone Stop the Waves?

3 Venice, Italy, has a dire water problem. Surrounded by its famous canals, the city has been sinking for centuries—leaving its priceless art treasures under water when the sea swells. The answer to the problem? In the Bible, Moses parted the Red Sea. Now, Project Moses may part the waters at Venice, using 300-ton hydraulic damns. Pumped with air to rise from the sea like giant beach balls, 79 of these dams will block raising waters to safeguard Venice. However, the project remains controversial. Studies are continuing to ensure these great dams (which might take until 2011 to complete) will really work—and at the same time not harm surrounding ecosystems.

4 What would happen if a dam didn't reach to the ocean floor? Wouldn't the waves just pass right under it? You'd think so. Yet "floating breakwaters" stop ocean waves—even though they don't touch the ocean bottom. Strangely, these wave-stoppers don't stop smooth oncoming water from passing through, but just waves.

Venice is in danger of flooding.

Photo: © iStockphoto.com/Roberto Cerruti

The secret? "Destructive interference."

5   Floating breakwaters resemble the lane buoys in swimming pools—except that each buoy is much larger, and layers of them (strung on sturdy lines) ride on each other. Each buoy exposes carefully shaped angles and recesses.

6   When waves enter the buoys, they must twist through. Impact and friction rob the waves of their energy, leaving the exiting water nearly calm. Amazingly, the buoys need only to extend a few wavelengths deep to stop moderate-size waves. Strung across an inlet, floating breakwaters can provide a calm harbor even when the sea is rough.

7   The technique is already at work. Floating breakwaters are reducing waves to slow coastline erosion at Redondo Beach, WA, as well as lowering the waves from passing boats on New York's Lake Ontario. In September 2003, floating breakwaters installed at the Navy's amphibious base near Norfolk, VA, withstood the furious wave forces of Hurricane Isabel.

8   To escape the waves, a ship might sail behind a **jetty**. But what if a ship could carry its own wave-stoppers anywhere it sailed? It sounds impossible, but RIBS, the Army Corps of Engineers' Rapidly Installed Breakwater System, does just that, making a safe harbor that ships can carry with them.

jetty
a pier or structure of stones, piles, or the like, projecting into the sea or other body of water to protect a harbor, deflect the current

Artist rendering of RIBS in use (left); field test of RIBS (above)

Images: US Army Engineer Research and Development Center

Can Anyone Stop the Waves?

9   Constructed from huge, floating, fabric beams, RIBS is towed behind a ship and then assembled to form a vee around the ship's hull. Specially designed drapes hanging from the beams into the water stop waves from entering, creating calm water around the boat. While RIBS could not hold back hurricane-size waves, it might help provide hurricane relief. Large ships carrying emergency supplies must often unload their cargo to smaller ships in mid-ocean. With RIBS, this transfer would be possible even in stormy seas.

10 "You'll never be able to control nature," MIT engineer Rafael L. Bras told *New York Times* reporters soon after the levees broke at New Orleans in 2005. "The best way is to understand how nature works and make it work in our favor." With wave barriers that move, and float, and even follow ships, creative engineers are surely trying just that.

Questions about the Text

If you need extra space, write any questions about the text in the space below. Be sure to identify the paragraph that sparked the question.

What Is This Article Mostly About?

Identify the most important information in the text. Write two to three sentences identifying what the text was mostly about.

Reading Passage for Lesson 15

Chasing the Storm

A WC-130J Super Hercules takes off during a hurricane tracking mission.

reconnaissance
a search made for useful military information in the field, especially by examining the ground

1. The official "Hurricane Hunters" are the Air Force Reserve's 53rd Weather **Reconnaissance Squadron**. They fly through the eyes of hurricanes and record information. The information helps the National Hurricane Center meteorologists improve the forecasts by up to 30%. How does this happen?

2. For each mission, the Hurricane Hunters fly through the eye of a hurricane multiple times. They pinpoint the center of the hurricane and whether the hurricane is strengthening or weakening. Also, instruments on the plane continually record the wind speed and direction. This information helps when forecasting the hurricane's track. The more accurate the forecast is, the less coastline will need to be evacuated. It costs about $1 million per mile to evacuate, so the information provided by the Hurricane Hunters is very valuable.

Photo: U.S. Air Force photo/Staff Sgt. Michael B. Keller

FOUNDATIONS • EXTREME WEATHER—LEVEL D

Chasing the Storm

Hurricane Hunters on their way to a hurricane

Hurricane Damage

3   Rain, wind, tornadoes, and storm surge related to hurricanes cause change to natural environments, damage to the human-built environment, and even loss of life. When a hurricane is over the ocean and far from land, wind and large waves created by the storm are a hazard for boats at sea. But with modern forecasting and warning systems, boats can steer clear of a hurricane. Before forecasting and warnings became common, hurricanes were the cause of many shipwrecks including several in the Bermuda Triangle, an area known for disappearing ships. Unlike boats, oil and gas platforms over the water are unable to move out of harms way and can be damaged by the fierce wind and waves.

4   When a hurricane approaches land, tremendous damage can occur in the built environment. The amount of damage depends both on the intensity of the storm and what it hits. A combination of winds, storm surge, and rain cause great damage to buildings, power lines, roads, and automobiles. During hurricane Katrina in

Photo: U.S. Air Force photo/Master Sgt. Jack Braden

2005 levees broke causing much of the city of New Orleans, LA to flood. The damage to the U.S. Gulf coast caused by Hurricane Katrina was the most costly in U.S. history.

5 Hurricanes cause many changes to the natural environment along a coast too. Sand is eroded from some coastal areas and deposited in others. The waves and storm surge are able to carry large rocks and even boulders. Many low-lying areas are flooded by storm surge. And strong winds and floods can thin or destroy forests.

Houses in Orange Beach, Alabama, a barrier island community before (top) and after (bottom) Hurricane Ivan, which hit the coast in September 2004.

Photo: USGS

Chasing the Storm

6 After a hurricane hits a coastal area, it can travel inland. At this point, the storm has typically weakened, but it can still cause serious damage. Torrential rains from the storm can cause flooding and mudslides.

7 It is estimated that 10,000 people die each year worldwide due to hurricanes and tropical storms. The majority of human deaths are caused by flooding. Because they can be very dangerous, it is important to look for hurricane warnings and to evacuate if it is recommended in your area. If you live in a hurricane prone area, visit the Hurricane Preparedness web site at the U.S. National Hurricane Center for tips on how to prepare for a hurricane.

Hurricane Hunters Chart

Saving Money	Saving Lives	Information about Research	Interesting Facts

Hurricane Advice

Based on what you have read about hurricanes, what would your advice be to someone who lives in a hurricane-prone area? Identify what they would need to be aware of and support your answers with evidence from the texts.

Video for Lesson 16

Hurricane Hunters

Hurricane Hunters prepare to go on a mission.

Transcript of "Hurricane Hunters" Video:

1. **Radio from aircraft:**
"John, how far north are we going to be going on the, uh, northbound track?"
"108 miles north of the eye"
"Ok—great."

2. **Narrator:** The job of a hurricane hunter is not for the faint at heart. These brave men and women must fly straight into one of the most destructive forces in nature.

3. **Narrator:** Hurricanes are born over the open ocean, and while satellites can track their movement, meteorologists and researchers need to sample the storms directly to get the most accurate information about them.

Photo: U.S. Air Force photo/Staff Sgt. Michael B. Keller

FOUNDATIONS • EXTREME WEATHER—LEVEL D | 95

Hurricane Hunters

4. **Narrator:** NOAA's hurricane hunter fleet includes two P-3 turboprop aircraft as well as a Gulfstream IV jet. The P-3s fly through the storm, encountering devastating winds that can be over 150 miles per hour. The jet can fly higher than the turboprops, gathering data from the upper atmosphere.

5. **Narrator:** Both planes have high tech equipment on board to get the job done, like radar and fixed probes that measure particles in the air.

6. **Narrator:** Scientists also deploy dropwindsondes, which parachute down through the hurricane to the ocean surface, sending back data on pressure, temperature, humidity, and wind.

7. **Narrator:** These measurements can help us understand the structure of a storm and the winds that are steering it. The data is used in computer models that help forecasters predict how intense the hurricane will be, and where and when it will strike land.

8. **Narrator:** Hurricane hunters take a literal look into the eye of a monster formed by nature. Their courage helps further science, which saves lives.

Reading Passage for Lesson 16

Restore Vital Hurricane Hunters Aircraft Operations

KATHY CASTOR
11TH DISTRICT, FLORIDA
COMMITTEE ON ARMED SERVICES
SUBCOMMITTEE ON TACTICAL AIR AND LAND
SUBCOMMITTEE ON EMERGING THREATS AND CAPABILITIES
COMMITTEE ON THE BUDGET
DEMOCRATIC STEERING AND POLICY COMMITTEE
ASSISTANT WHIP

Congress of the United States
House of Representatives
Washington, DC 20515–0911

WASHINGTON OFFICE:
137 CANNON BUILDING
WASHINGTON, DC 20515
(202) 225–3376

DISTRICT OFFICE:
4144 NORTH ARMENIA AVENUE
SUITE 300
TAMPA, FL 33607
(813) 871-2817
www.castor.house.gov

August 26, 2011

The Honorable John Boehner
Speaker
U.S. House of Representatives
H-232
U.S. Capitol
Washington, DC 20515

The Honorable Hal Rogers
Chairman
Appropriations Committee
H-307
U.S. Capitol
Washington, DC 20515

The Honorable Frank Wolf
Chairman
Commerce, Justice, Science, and Related Agencies Subcommittee
H-309
U.S. Capitol
Washington, DC 20515

Re: Restore Vital Hurricane Hunters Aircraft Operations

Dear Speaker Boehner, Chairman Rogers, and Chairman Wolf:

1. I respectfully request that the Appropriations Committee work to restore the devastating cuts to the Hurricane Hunters Aircraft Operations under the National Oceanic and Atmospheric Administration in the proposed 2012 Commerce, Justice, Science Appropriations bill. As you are aware, the bill is likely to come to the **floor** for **amendment** this fall.

> **Speaker**
> the person in charge of political debates in some legislatures

> **appropriations**
> amount of money kept separate to use for a particular purpose, especially by a government

> **floor**
> a place where discussions or debates take place, especially in a legislature

> **amendment**
> a change made to a law or agreement

Restore Vital Hurricane Hunters Aircraft Operations

asset
a valuable or useful person or thing

deficit
the amount by which a sum of money is less than the required or expected amount

degradation
changing to a lower or less respected state

2. For communities across the country facing the threat of devastation from hurricanes, there is no greater **asset** than information. Accurate and timely information can mean the difference between life and death. That is why I am so concerned about the proposed cuts to National Oceanic and Atmospheric Administration's budget, particularly the amount from the aircraft operations. The Commerce, Justice, Science Appropriations bill passed by the committee includes a forty percent cut to the vital hurricane hunters operations. I plan to offer an amendment to restore this funding when this bill comes to the floor.

3. We must do everything we can to address our debt and **deficit**, however we must balance it in a way that recognizes the needs of communities. The costs of the hurricane hunters operations pale in comparison to the lives and money saved with the increasingly accurate predictions that come from these flights out of MacDill Air Force Base. James Franklin, head of forecast operations for the National Hurricane Center said, "If those flights were to stop for whatever reason, there would be a **degradation** in our forecasts for storms threatening the United States." The aircraft at MacDill are unique and crucial to the research being done in improving hurricane predictions. Improved predictions not only save lives, but can save millions of dollars in unnecessary business closures and **evacuations**.

4. We have talented people working at MacDill to develop new science and advancements that have made tracking of hurricanes and storms so much more accurate than in the past. I have attached an article that outlines some of their successes, including narrowing the cone of uncertainty by as much as 50 percent in the past decade. Unfortunately, without the funding for the aircraft, this research will be in jeopardy. As Frank Marks, research meteorologist and director of the NOAA/Atlantic Oceanographic

Meteorological Laboratory Hurricane Research Division, said, "take them out of the equation and our research is dead in the water."

5   We must continue to support the research and advancements of the hurricane hunters operations. I urge you to support my amendment to restore funding to this vital program.

Sincerely,

Kathy Castor
United States Representative
Florida – District 11

Pronoun Practice

3   We must do everything we can to address our debt and deficit, however we must balance it in a way that recognizes the needs of communities. The costs of the hurricane hunters operations pale in comparison to the lives and money saved with the increasingly accurate predictions that come from these flights out of MacDill Air Force Base. James Franklin, head of forecast operations for the National Hurricane Center said, "If those flights were to stop for whatever reason, there would be a degradation in our forecasts for storms threatening the United States." The aircraft at MacDill are unique and crucial to the research being done in improving hurricane predictions. Improved predictions not only save lives, but can save millions of dollars in unnecessary business closures and evacuations.

4   We have talented people working at MacDill to develop new science and advancements that have made tracking of hurricanes and storms so much more accurate than in the past. I have attached an article that outlines some of their successes, including narrowing the cone of uncertainty by as much as 50 percent in the past decade. Unfortunately, without the funding for the aircraft, this research will be in jeopardy. As Frank Marks, research meteorologist and director of the NOAA/Atlantic Oceanographic Meteorological Laboratory Hurricane Research Division, said, "take them out of the equation and our research is dead in the water."

Lessons 17–18

Library Research

Work with your group to research the natural disaster you have chosen.

Make sure you find answers to the questions below. When your research is complete, make a graphic on chart paper that captures the information you have collected.

- Where and when did the weather-related natural disaster take place?
- What kind of damage did the weather-related natural disaster cause?
- Were there any special circumstances that contributed to the damage or lessened the damage? If so, what were they?
- Were any lessons learned from the natural disaster? If so, what?

Photo: © iStockphoto.com/Eric Hood

Evaluating Websites

Domain	Purpose
.com	Commercial, hosted by a company
.edu	Educational use
.mil	Military branch of the government
.org	Nonprofit organization
.net	Usually an Internet provider
.gov	Government website

Questions to ask:

- Is there an author?

- What is the last date the website was updated?

- How detailed is the information?

- Do the links work and do they include useful information?

- Are there any biases?

- Are there citations?

- Are there errors?

Research Notes

Use the space below to write notes about your research.

Notes on Other Presentations

Natural Disaster:

_____
_____
_____
_____
_____

Natural Disaster:

_____
_____
_____
_____
_____

Natural Disaster:

_____
_____
_____
_____
_____

Natural Disaster:

_____
_____
_____
_____
_____

Natural Disaster:

_____
_____
_____
_____
_____

Natural Disaster:

_____
_____
_____
_____
_____

Reading Passage 1 for Lesson 19

Coldest Place—Antarctica

A Really "Cool" Place to Be a Scientist

1. You want to talk about world records; Antarctica is the land of extremes. It is the coldest, windiest, and highest continent anywhere on earth. With an average elevation about 7,544 ft/2,300 meters above sea level it is the highest continent. Even though it is covered in ice it receives some of the least amount of rainfall, getting just slightly more rainfall than the Sahara Desert, making it the largest **desert** on earth. Most people have the misconception that a desert is a hot, dry, sandy, lifeless place, but the true definition of a desert is any geographical location that receives very, very little rainfall. Even though there's ice on the ground in Antarctica, that ice has been there for a *very long time*.

Photo: © iStockphoto.com
Illustration: Adapted from iStockphoto.com/Bubaone

Coldest Place—Antarctica

indigenous
produced, growing, living, or occurring naturally in a particular region or environment; native

inaccessibility
not being available when needed; unapproachable

2   Antarctica is the only continent that has never had an **indigenous** population of humans because it has always been such an extreme environment. Just the boat ride getting to the continent is over the most treacherous seas anywhere in the world. The **inaccessibility** of the place and the lack of reliable food and means for constructing shelter have kept humans away for thousands of years. But the new technologies developed over the last 200 years made it possible for people to reach these icy shores to explore and study the Antarctic for the first time in human history.

3   Since there are no people who claim Antarctica as their homeland, exploration of the continent has been shared by all nations of the world. Scientists from all over the world—Russia, Japan, the United States, United Kingdom, Australia, New Zealand, South America, and many others—come to this place in an internationally cooperative agreement to study the truly unique qualities of Antarctica. Many scientific stations have been constructed on Antarctica to provide shelter and supplies for scientists doing fieldwork there.

McMurdo Station, a research center in Antarctica

Photo: © iStockphoto.com/Jeff Samuels

Satellite image of Antarctica shows ice sheets off the coast of the continent.

4   Some scientists actually live on Antarctica for part of the year to conduct their research. Very few scientists stay there more than six months at a time. The sun rises and sets only once a year at the South Pole, which means there are six months of daylight, followed by six months of darkness. During the winter when there is no sun, the Antarctic becomes an even more hostile place to be—colder than cold, BONE-CHILLING cold, and no daylight. Can you imagine living in darkness 24 hours a day?

Antarctic Ice—The Ultimate Cool

5   Many scientists study Antarctic ice because it is more than just ice. It has accumulated over time, layer upon layer, building up over the millennia to create a type of **sedimentary** rock. Yes, rock. Ice crystals can be considered a type of mineral, and glacial ice is composed of crystals of the "mineral" water. Just like sedimentary rock is created over time by the repeated layering of particles of clay or sand, glacial ice builds up over millions of years by the build up of snow that never melts.

Photo: USGS, Landsat Image Mosaic of Antarctica

> **sedimentary**
> *formed by or from deposits of sediment*

Coldest Place—Antarctica

geologic time
the time of the physical formation and development of Earth, especially prior to human history

6   Scientists drill down deep into the ice with a drill that works kind of like a cookie cutter, only it cuts out some really deep cookies of ice. These core samples contain many layers of ice that represent what the earth's atmosphere was like at the time each layer of ice was formed. By studying the layers of ice in the core samples scientists can learn about how the earth's atmosphere has changed over **geologic time**.

7   In the winter time the ocean around Antarctica freezes for thousands of miles in all directions. This vast expanse of ice surrounding the already immense Antarctic ice sheet covers over eleven million square kilometers. The annual freezing of the ocean around Antarctica generates deep ocean currents worldwide. Differences in ocean temperature are what cause weather all over the globe. Some scientists fear that if the global climate gets too warm or too cold it could affect the formation of Antarctic ice, changing the climate as we know it all over the world.

Reading Passage 2 for Lesson 19

Hottest Temperature—El Azizia, Libya

Libyan desert

How Hot Is Hot?

1. There are many places on earth that are plenty hot—record-breaking hot. In fact, there's a good chance on the day the record-breaking temperature of 136° F/57.8° C was recorded by a meteorological station in El Azizia in 1922, there were other places hundreds of miles away that were even hotter. In all likelihood, this record temperature has been exceeded since then in many places on earth, but we have no official records of the temperatures. It is important to note that when atmospheric temperatures are recorded it is not the *surface* temperature, where it can sometimes reach 150° F/66° C, but rather the *air* temperature at about 5 feet (1.6 m) above the surface in an enclosed shelter. Of course, it's important that the temperature sensor is not exposed to direct sunlight—the shelter is **louvered** to permit airflow across the sensor. Most humans don't 'hang out'

louvered
supplied with a series of slanted fixed or movable fins that allow an opening for ventilation

Photo: © iStockphoto.com/Kurt Drubbel
Illustration: Adapted from iStockphoto.com/Bubaone

FOUNDATIONS • EXTREME WEATHER—LEVEL D | 109

Hottest Temperature—El Azizia, Libya

Gobi desert

where some of the hottest temperatures on earth are regularly experienced so there aren't a lot of meteorological stations in these places to reliably record extreme temperatures.

Desert Lands

2. As big as the earth is, over two thirds of its surface is covered in water from the oceans. The remaining one-third of the earth's surface is exposed as dry land for us to live on, but a third of that dry land is *really* dry. In fact, it's inhospitable desert. Much of the deserts in the world are clustered between 5 to 30 degrees north and south of the equator, in what are called **subtropical** *zones*. Scientists have theorized that these desert belts are due to two things:

1) Heat

2) Lack of moisture

Photo: © iStockphoto.com/Viktor Glupov

3   Duh? Anybody who's ever been outside on a hot summer day, all day, knows *that*. Just about every continent on earth that is **inhabited** by humans experiences seasonal weather changes, with a distinct winter and summer. Just because there's hot, dry weather during the summer, doesn't mean that where you live is going to turn into a desert. What makes the desert so hot and dry is the climatic conditions that are sustained almost continually, year round. Any part of the world that's hot and dry for long enough periods throughout the year won't be able to support much plant or animal life. Living things need water to survive.

Death Valley, California

inhabited
occupied; lived in or on

Why Is It so Dry All the Time?

4   First, the air in the earth's atmosphere is warmest around the equator (because the sun reaches the earth at a direct 90° angle) so that warmer air rises and flows north and south of the equator. As the air "piles" up in the northern and southern latitudes, these zones of "piled-high" warm air become permanent high-pressure

Photo: © iStockphoto.com/Keith Kiska

Hottest Temperature—El Azizia, Libya

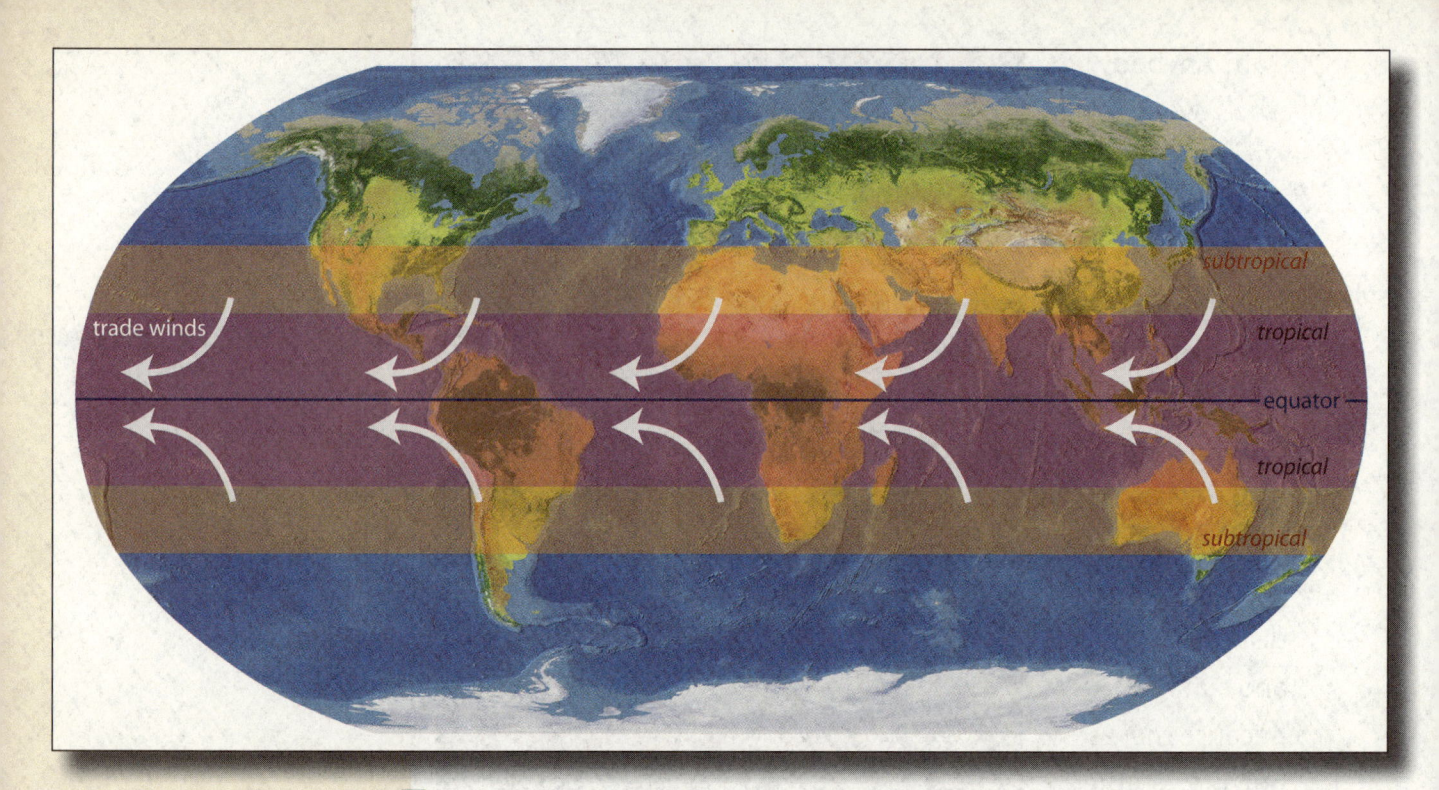

[Map showing world with subtropical, tropical, equator, tropical, subtropical zones labeled; arrows indicating trade winds]

zones. As the air at the "bottom of the pile" descends toward the earth it gets warmed up even more. Because this descending warm air has no clouds (i.e., condensing water vapor), that allows the burning sun to go right through the air and heat the land mass below even more. Hence, extreme heat. Warm air can hold a lot more moisture (water vapor) than colder air. Unless this really warm air contacts some much cooler air (or cooler land mass), there's nothing to coax the moisture out of the air in the form of precipitation (rain, fog). Hence, lack of moisture.

What Goes Around, Comes Around

5   This hot air moves northward and southward of the equator, almost continuously in the form of reliable winds called the Trade Winds. As these warm winds circulate back around towards the equator they rise into the upper atmosphere again, cooling. The water vapor in the cooling air mass condenses and rains, and rains and rains all over the equator in the Tropical zones. All this

Map: Adapted from iStockphoto.com/Jan Rysavy

rain makes the landmass around the equator the lushest, wettest, most densely forested in the world (plants love water!). It's ironic that the wettest and hottest places in the world occur within just a few thousand miles of each other.

6   Though the hottest place in the world, El Azizia, is a desert, not all deserts are hot. Antarctica, for example, is the driest continent on earth, getting less than 4 in/10 cm of precipitation a year. What characterizes or defines a desert is the lack of precipitation—less than 10 in/25.4 cm per year. In the Antarctic, there is very little precipitation in the form of rain or snow. Even though there's water, water everywhere it's locked up in the form of ice.

Coldest and Hottest Places Venn Diagram

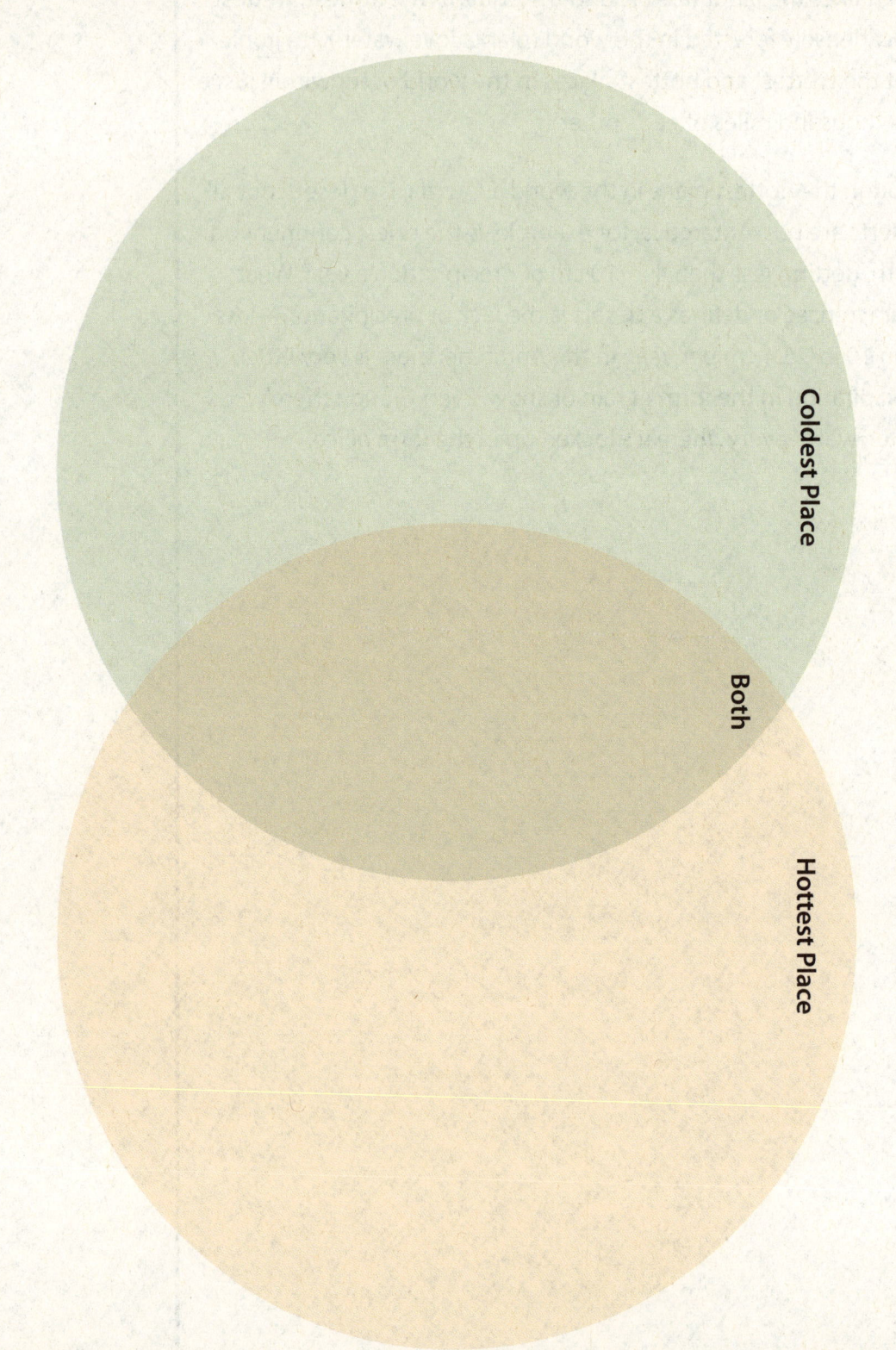

Coldest Place

Both

Hottest Place

Reading Passage 1 for Lesson 20

Atacama Desert—The World's Driest Desert

Atacama Desert, Chile

1. While deserts are by definition, places where rain is scarce, there is only one area on this earth—the central portion of Chile's Atacama Desert, where it never ever rained—at least since humans started keeping a record—about 400 years ago!

2. The most amazing part is, that this 600-mile stretch of land lies right alongside Chile's coast, next to the biggest body of water on Earth—The Pacific Ocean. Though drier than all other deserts, the temperature in the Atacama Desert is quite cool, ranging from 0–25 degrees Celsius, thanks to its high altitude.

3. The reason for the extremely arid weather is its location, in the *rain shadow*, smack between the Andes Mountains and the Chilean Coast Range.

Photo: © iStockphoto.com/José Carlos Pires Pereira
Illustration: Adapted from iStockphoto.com/Bubaone

FOUNDATIONS • EXTREME WEATHER—LEVEL D

Atacama Desert—The World's Driest Desert

4   The warm tropical air that brings rain to the South American rainforests are prevented from coming across thanks to the high Andes—Instead, the high altitude forces the air to cool and precipitate right on the mountains. By the time it rolls on the other side the warm air holds on to whatever moisture it has, instead of falling on the ground below.

5   While the weather makes it almost impossible for anything to survive, the area's unusual landscape has made it a goldmine for scientists and astronomers.

6   The arid cold weather is the closest substitute for the weather on Mar's giving NASA scientists the perfect testing grounds for any equipment they wish to send to the Red Planet.

7   Also, thanks to the high altitude, nearly non-existent cloud cover, dry air, lack of light pollution and radio **interferences** from cities, the area is perfect for astronomy observations.

8   Already home to two major European observatories, a third dubbed ALMA, a collaboration between Europe, Japan, United States and South America, is currently underway. As would be expected, the area is also popular among filmmakers looking to film scenes on 'Mars'. However, while the Atacama Desert maybe the 'driest' desert in the World, it is only the second driest region—the winner? Icy Antarctica!

> **interferences**
> jumbling of radio signals, caused by the reception of undesired ones

Radio telescopes in the Atacama Desert

Photo: © iStockphoto.com/Rocco Montoya

Wettest Place—Cherrapunji, India

1. Cherrapunji is about 90–100 kilometers away from my home. It sits on the southern tip of the Khasi Hills, facing Bangladesh. Cherrapunji's yearly average rainfall stands at 463 inches. Can you imagine how much that is? New York's average annual rainfall is 47 inches. So here it rains ten times as much as it does in New York!

2. The cliffs of Cherrapunji receive heavy rainfall due to **monsoon** winds blowing from the Bay of Bengal. Thus, the region is home to extremely wet weather.

3. Cherrapunji receives both the Southwest and Northeast monsoon showers, which give it a single monsoon season. It lies on the windward side of the Khasi Hills.

Wettest Place—Cherrapunji, India

Monsoon clouds over India

Cause of Extremely High Rainfall

4   Cherrapunji receives rains from the Bay of Bengal arm of the Indian Summer Monsoon. The monsoon clouds fly unhindered over the plains of Bangladesh for about 400 km. Suddenly, they hit the Khasi Hills, which rise abruptly out of the plains, reaching a height of about 1370 m.

5   The geography of the hills, with its many deep valleys, channels the low-flying (150–300 m) moisture-laden clouds. The clouds move from a wide area into a narrow one to converge over Cherrapunji.

6   The winds push the rain clouds through these gorges and up the steep slopes. The rapid ascent of the clouds into the upper atmosphere hastens the cooling and helps vapors to condense. Most of Cherrapunji's rain is the result of this phenomenon of air being lifted as a large body of water vapor.

Photo: © iStockphoto.com/Ajay Bhaskar

Driest and Wettest Places Venn Diagram

Wettest Place

Both

Driest Place

LESSON 20 FOUNDATIONS • EXTREME WEATHER—LEVEL D

Where Would You Rather Live?

Based on what you have read about the coldest, hottest, driest, and wettest places on Earth, if you had to choose, where would you rather live and why? Support your answer with evidence from the texts.

Reading Passage for Lessons 21–22

Death Valley Weather and Climate

1. Death Valley is famous as the hottest and driest place in North America. Summer temperatures often top 120°F (49°C) in the shade with overnight lows dipping into the 90s°F (mid 30s°C). Average rainfall is less than 2 inches (5 cm), a fraction of what most deserts receive. Occasional thunderstorms, especially in late summer, can cause flashfloods.

2. In contrast to the extremes of summertime, winter and spring are very pleasant. Winter daytime temperatures are mild in the low elevations, with cool nights that only occasionally reach freezing. Higher elevations are cooler than the low valley. Temperatures drop 3 to 5°F (2–3°C) with every thousand vertical feet (approx. 300 m). Sunny skies are the norm in Death Valley, but winter storms and summer monsoons can bring cloud cover and rain. Wind is common in the desert, especially in the spring. Dust storms can suddenly blow up with approaching cold fronts.

Photo: © iStockphoto.com/Jon Larson
Illustration: Adapted from iStockphoto.com/Bubaone

Death Valley Weather and Climate

Why Is Death Valley's Weather so Extreme?

Why so Dry?

3   Winter storms moving inland from the Pacific Ocean must pass over mountain ranges to continue east. As the clouds rise up they cool and the moisture condenses to fall as rain or snow on the western side of the ranges. By the time the clouds reach the mountain's east side they no longer have as much available moisture, creating a dry "**rainshadow**". Four major mountain ranges lie between Death Valley and the ocean, each one adding to an increasingly drier rainshadow effect.

Why so Hot?

4   The depth and shape of Death Valley influence its summer temperatures. The valley is a long, narrow basin 282 feet (86 m) below sea level, yet is walled by high, steep mountain ranges. The clear, dry air and sparse plant cover allow sunlight to heat the desert surface. Heat radiates back from the rocks and soil, and then becomes trapped in the valley's depths. Summer nights provide little relief as overnight lows may only dip into the 85°F to 95°F (30°C to 35°C) range. Heated air rises, yet is trapped by the high valley walls, is cooled and recycled back down to the valley floor. These pockets of descending air are only slightly cooler than the surrounding hot air. As they descend, they are compressed and heated even more by the low elevation air pressure. These moving masses of super heated air blow through the valley creating extreme high temperatures.

A view of Telescope Peak on the west side of Death Valley. The mountains contribute to the rainshadow effect.

Photo: © iStockphoto.com/Harry Thomas

How Extreme Is Death Valley's Climate?

Record Temperatures

5   The hottest air temperature ever recorded in Death Valley (Furnace Creek) was 134°F (57°C) on July 10, 1913. During the heat wave that peaked with that record, five consecutive days reached 129° F (54°C) or above. Death Valley held the record for the hottest place on earth until 1922. Oddly enough, 1913 was also the year that saw Death Valley's coldest temperature. On January 8 the temperature dropped to 15°F (-10°C) at Furnace Creek.

Salt flats near Furnace Creek

Longest Summers

6   The greatest number of consecutive days with a maximum temperature of 100° F or above was 154 days in the summer of 2001. The summer of 1996 had 40 days over 120° F, and 105 days over 110° F. The summer of 1917 had 43 consecutive days with a high temperature of 120° F or above.

Photo: © iStockphoto.com/Steve Geer

Death Valley Weather and Climate

Highest Ground Temperatures

7   The highest ground temperature recorded was 201° F at Furnace Creek on July 15, 1972. The maximum air temperature for that day was 128° F.

Dry as a Bone

8   No rain was recorded in the years of 1929 and 1953. The driest stretch on record was only 0.64 inches (1.6 cm) of rain over a 40-month period in 1931 to 1934. Weather data was compiled from park and National Weather Service record summaries for the years 1911 through 2007 for Furnace Creek in Death Valley, California.

Geology

9   Death Valley National Park showcases the subtle beauty and uniqueness of desert environments. What events conspired to create Death Valley? Why is the landscape so varied, and so extreme? Badwater Basin contains the lowest point in North America, at 282 feet below sea level, yet it lies in the afternoon shadow of 11,049-foot Telescope Peak. This rugged **topography**, as well as sand dunes, craters, and flood-carved canyons, indicate that Death Valley has experienced a lengthy and complex geologic history.

> **topography**
> the features of a particular area of land, such as hills, rivers, and roads

Badwater Basin—the lowest point in North America

Photo: © iStockphoto.com/fotoVoyager

Ancient Seas

10   Death Valley's rocks, structure and landforms offer a wealth of information about what the area may have looked like in the past. It is apparent that there has not always been a valley here. Death Valley's oldest rocks, formed at least 1.7 billion years ago, are so severely altered that their history is almost undecipherable. Rocks dating from 500 million years ago, however, paint a clearer picture. The limestones and sandstones found in the Funeral and Panamint Mountains indicate that this area was the site of a warm, shallow sea throughout most of the Paleozoic Era (542–251 million years ago).

Zabriskie Point, at the edge of the Funeral Mountains

Warped Mountains

11   Time passed and the sea began to slowly recede to the west as land was pushed up. This uplift was due to movement occurring far beneath the Earth's surface. Scientists have discovered that the Earth's crust is composed of interconnected sections, or plates. Death Valley lies near the boundary between two of these plates. As the plates slowly move in relation to each other, compressional forces gradually fold, warp and fracture the brittle crust. This widespread rock deformation and faulting occurred through most of the Mesozoic Era (251–65.5 million years ago). While the Rocky Mountains and the Sierra Nevada formed, active mountain building alternated with times when erosion prevailed, worked to breaking down the mountains that had formed.

Photo: © iStockphoto.com/Paul Lemke

Death Valley Weather and Climate

Traveling Volcanoes

12. The next phase in Death Valley's development was primarily influenced by volcanic activity that spanned much of the Tertiary Period (65.5–2 million years ago). As fault movement and mountain building stretched the land surface, the crust was weakened. Hot, molten material beneath the surface welled up and erupted at these weak points. The seething volcanoes first appeared to the northeast, in Nevada, and blanketed the Death Valley region with numerous layers of ash and cinders. The topography then consisted of gently rolling hills, perhaps similar to the present-day Skidoo area. Over time, the center of volcanic activity moved progressively westward, finally producing a chain of volcanoes from Furnace Creek to Shoshone, burying the ancient rocks of the Black Mountains. Secondary results of the ash and cinder eruptions include the vivid colors of the Artist's Palette and Death Valley's famous borate mineral deposits.

Artist's Palette, Panamint Mountains, Death Valley National Park

Photo: © iStockphoto.com/Dean Pennala

Basin and Range

13 Approximately three million years ago, the dynamics of **crustal movement** changed, and Death Valley proper began to form. At that time, compression was replaced by extensional forces. This "pulling apart" of Earth's crust allowed large blocks of land to slowly slide past one another along faults, forming alternating valleys and mountain ranges. Badwater Basin, the Death Valley salt pan and the Panamint mountain range comprise one block that is rotating eastward as a structural unit. The valley floor has been steadily slipping downward, **subsiding** along the fault that lies at the base of the Black Mountains. Subsidence continues today. Evidence of this can be seen in the fresh fault scarps exposed near Badwater.

Erosion and Deposition

14 **Concurrent** with the subsidence has been slow but continuous erosion. Water carries rocks, gravel, sand and silt down from surrounding hills and deposits them on the valley floor. Beneath Badwater lies more than 11,000 feet of accumulated sediment and salts.

crustal movement
movement resulting from or causing deformation of Earth's crust

subsiding
sinking or falling to the bottom

concurrent
occurring or existing simultaneously or side by side

Salt from deposit in Death Valley

Photo: © iStockphoto.com/Branko Habjan

Death Valley Weather and Climate

Ubehebe Crater

Lost Lakes

15 In addition to structural changes, Death Valley has been subjected to major climatic changes throughout the past three million years. During North America's last major Ice Age, the valley was part of a system of large lakes. The lakes disappeared approximately 10,000 years ago, evaporating as the climate warmed. As the lakes evaporated, vast fields of salt deposits were left behind. A smaller, now vanished, lake system occupied the basin floor about 3000 years ago.

Yesterday's Volcano

16 Signs of recent volcanic activity exist in northern Death Valley at Ubehebe Crater. Caused by violent steam explosions, the craters may have formed as recently as 300 years ago when hot, molten material came in contact with groundwater. These large depressions show that Death Valley's geology is dynamic and ever changing.

Photo: © iStockphoto.com/Glenn Nagel

Shape of the Future

17 Death Valley's landscape has been changing for millions of years. It is changing now, and will continue to change long after we have departed. Erosion slowly carves away at the ancient rock formations, reshaping the surface of the land. The basin continues to subside and the mountains rise ever higher. It is interesting to imagine, but impossible to predict, the future of Death Valley.

Desert Comparison Chart

	Desert			
	Antarctica	Atacama	El Azizia	Death Valley
Dry?				
Hot?				
Record Temperature				
Record Surface Temperature				
Precipitation				
Altitude				

Reflection

Why did the authors not include all the information for this chart in their writings?

_____
_____
_____
_____
_____

130 | LITERACY NAVIGATOR

LESSON 21

Death Valley Timeline

Tertiary Period (65.5–2 million years ago)

Mesozoic Era (251–65.5 million years ago)

Paleozoic Era (542–251 million years ago)

Changing Landscape

Based on what we have read today, what are the elements that can change the Earth? How would your area look different if the lakes dried up, a volcano erupted, or a mountain sprang up over night? How are the places we live dependent on the landscape around us?

Reading Passage for Lesson 23

The Dust Bowl

1. The most visible evidence of how dry the 1930s became was the dust storm. Tons of **topsoil** were blown off barren fields and carried in storm clouds for hundreds of miles. Technically, the driest region of the Plains—southeastern Colorado, southwest Kansas and the **panhandles** of Oklahoma and Texas—became known as the Dust Bowl, and many dust storms started there. But the entire region, and eventually the entire country, was affected. The Dust Bowl got its name after Black Sunday, April 14, 1935. More and more dust storms had been blowing up in the years leading up to that day. In 1932, 14 dust storms were recorded on the Plains. In 1933, there were 38 storms. By 1934, it was estimated that 100 million acres of farmland had lost all or most of the topsoil to the winds. By April 1935, there had been weeks of dust storms, but the cloud that appeared on the horizon that Sunday was the worst. Winds were clocked at 60 mph. Then it hit.

panhandles
a relatively narrow strip of land projecting from some larger area, such as a state

Photo: NOAA George E. Marsh Album
Illustration: Adapted from iStockphoto.com/Bubaone

The Dust Bowl

2. "The impact is like a shovelful of fine sand flung against the face," Avis D. Carlson wrote in a *New Republic* article. "People caught in their own yards grope for the doorstep. Cars come to a standstill, for no light in the world can penetrate that swirling murk . . . We live with the dust, eat it, sleep with it, watch it strip us of possessions, and the hope of possessions. It is becoming Real."

A forlorn farmer leans into a dust storm.

3. The day after Black Sunday, an Associated Press reporter used the term "Dust Bowl" for the first time. "Three little words achingly familiar on the Western farmer's tongue, rule life in the dust bowl of the continent—if it rains." The term stuck and was used by radio reporters and writers, in private letters and public speeches. In the central and northern plains, dust was everywhere.

4. The impact of the Dust Bowl was felt all over the U.S. During the same April as Black Sunday, 1935, one of FDR's advisors, Hugh Hammond Bennett, was in Washington D.C. on his way to testify before Congress about the need for soil conservation legislation. A dust storm arrived in Washington all the way from the Great Plains. As a dusty gloom spread over the nation's capital and blotted out the sun, Bennett explained, "This, gentlemen, is what I have been talking about." Congress passed the Soil Conservation Act that same year.

Photo: NOAA, NOAA's National Weather Service (NWS) Collection

Aerial view of the beginning of a dust storm over the prairie lands east of Denver, Colorado.

No Water, No Crops

5   It probably sounds too obvious to say it—when rainfall in a region drops, crops won't grow, animals that are fed by the crops will suffer, and the economy of a region or an entire country will suffer as well. Everyone knows that plants need water to grow—as well as nutrients, sun and air. But the drought years of the 1930s forced individual farmers and lawmakers at all levels of government to face fundamental questions. What kind of agriculture can be practiced in a semi-arid environment? And how can we restore land that farming practices had damaged and avoid damaging the land in the future?

6   The statistics tell the story:

- Normally, the state of Nebraska averages around 20 inches of rainfall a year.

- In 1930, Nebraska got 22 inches of rain, and the state's corn crop averaged 25 bushels per acre.

Photo: NOAA, NOAA's National Weather Service (NWS) Collection

The Dust Bowl

- In 1934, Nebraska saw the driest year on record with only 14.5 inches of rainfall. The state's corn crop dropped even more to only 6.2 bushels per acre.

Depression refers to the Great Depression, from 1929 through the 1930s, when there was a worldwide economic depression and mass unemployment

7   In other words, between 1930 and 1934 rainfall dropped 27.5 percent, and as a result corn crop yields dropped over 75 percent. Those living on the Great Plains saw the effects of the drought first hand. LeRoy Hankel can tell you how his crops did each year during the **Depression**, even after all these years. These dramatic effects caused the leaders of agricultural planning in the U.S. to consider fundamental changes in farming on the plains. The heads of all of the New Deal agricultural and relief agencies issued a "Report of the Great Plains Drought Area Committee" in August 1936.

8   In the report, they said that the Dust Bowl was caused not just by the dry weather but also by unwise farming practices. Earlier settlers plowed under the natural tall grasses that covered the plains and planted crops they had planted in the wetter East. When the drought came, the crops failed, the ground was uncovered and the incessant winds produced the dust storms. Government planners wrote that periods of drought like the 1930s were likely to occur again and that "the agricultural economy of the Great Plains will become increasingly unstable and unsafe . . . unless over-cropping, over-grazing and improper farm methods are prevented . . . The future of the region must depend, therefore, on the degree to which farming practices conform to natural conditions."

Photo: NOAA, NOAA's National Weather Service (NWS) Collection

A South Dakota farm blown away during the Dust Bowl years.

9   Helen Bolton remembers how their corn was fine one day and dried out the next. She and her husband used their anticipated crop yields to buy a tractor. When the crops failed, they were in trouble. Birdie Farr remembers when her husband's father lost his horse and cattle ranch in the Nebraska sand hills. With little rain, there was no grass in the pastures for livestock.

10 Farmers are optimistic. It's natural for them to push the limits, to try to raise a crop where crops haven't been raised before. But they can't control nature. They can't make it rain. And so the challenge is to find crops that are adapted to the specific region they live in, whether that's in the humid East or the dry places of the Plains and the West.

Photo: NOAA, NOAA's National Weather Service (NWS) Collection

The Dust Bowl

Oklahoma farmer and sons walking in the face of a dust storm.

Calling Off School for Dust

11   Each winter, students all across the North secretly—or openly—hope for snowstorms so that school will be called off. During the Depression, schools across the Plains sent students home because of the dust storms. Some school administrators were worried about what might happen to the students' health. There had been cases of "dust pneumonia" where dust clogged up the lungs just like the disease. Other administrators and teachers, especially in the southern Plains, knew that people had gotten lost in dust storms when visibility went to zero. Don McGinley remembers being let out of the Ogallala, Nebraska, school because of a dust storm. It was so bad that his mother thought the world might be coming to an end. In *Telling Tales Out of School*, a book by the National Retired Teachers Association, Taleta Elfeldt says, "One day in March 1934, my beginners were busy reading. All of a sudden there was total darkness. It was as though a huge curtain had been drawn around our building . . . I realized a dust storm had hit because soon the room was filled with a 'fog of dust' . . . We teachers walked home holding wet towels over our faces in order to breathe." Other rural teachers talked about lighting lanterns

Photo: Arthur Rothstein, USDA Natural Resources Conservation Service in the middle of the day so that children could see to recite their lessons. And sometimes, children were kept in the schoolhouse all night to make sure they wouldn't get lost walking home or be overcome by the dust. The dust was dangerous, and schools were taking no chances.

Red Dust from Oklahoma

12 The soil in the northern Great Plains is black, rich with organic material and humus that makes it a good medium for growing plants. And so, you'd expect the dust in the air to be the same basic color, black or gray. But in the 1930s, people all over the country saw red dust blanketing their homes, towns and farms.

13 Millie Opitz remembers the red dust rolling in. She learned later that it came from Oklahoma. And trying to clean it up left her rags red. The dust was red because the soils in Oklahoma—particularly in the panhandle of western Oklahoma—contain a lot of iron in them. Iron minerals, like hematite and ferrihydrite, will oxidize or rust, particularly in dry climates. That oxidation produces the distinctive red color of the soil and of the dust storms.

A wall of dust approaching a Kansas town.

Photo: NOAA, NOAA's National Weather Service (NWS) Collection

The Dust Bowl

A ranch house in South Dakota saved from burial by a wooden fence.

14. Dust from Oklahoma was blown as far north as Canada and as far East as the Atlantic Ocean. Delbert and Alvin Apetz remember the red dust and how tumbleweeds blew into fencerows, catching dust drifts behind them and threatening to cover the fences. Helen Bolton remembers how hot it got in the middle of those summers. Temperatures soared to over 100 degrees F day after day. Night after night, it would still be in the 80s well into the evening, making it uncomfortable to sleep—especially in the days before air conditioning. Farm families didn't even have electricity so they could run fans at night. Some people moved outdoors or into a basement, if they were lucky enough to have one. Others, like Helen Bolton, hung wet sheets around the bed in the hopes that the water evaporating from the sheets would cool the room.

Photo: NOAA, NOAA's National Weather Service (NWS) Collection

The Dust Bowl Web

The Dust Bowl

Letter from the Dust Bowl

Think about what it was like at this time in the United States: drought, dust storms, no air conditioning. Pretend you live in this part of the country at this time in our history. Write a letter to a friend in New York describing what your life is like, be sure to include information based on the text you read today.

Reading Passage for Lesson 24

China's Growing Deserts Are Suffocating Korea

Seoul, South Korea, on a hazy day

1. School was called off throughout much of this sprawling city last Monday because of inclement weather. It was not a freak spring snowstorm, a heat wave or torrential rains. Rather, it was an immense cloud of dust that blew in from China's fast-spreading deserts, about 750 miles away.

2. It hid Seoul from view throughout the morning, obscuring the sunrise just as surely as the heaviest of fogs. Clinics overflowed with patients complaining of breathing problems, drugstores experienced a run on cough medicines and face masks that supposedly filter the air, and parks and outdoor malls were nearly empty of pedestrians.

China's Growing Deserts Are Suffocating Korea

Dust blows from China across the Korean peninsula.

3   With the arrival of the huge dust storms for the third consecutive year, Koreans have begun to grimly resign themselves to the addition of an unwelcome fifth season—already dubbed the season of yellow dust—to the usual four seasons that any temperate country knows.

4   Like the **harmattan** in West Africa, when skies throughout that region turn a soupy gray for weeks at a time because of seasonal wind patterns that bring airborne dust southward from the Sahara, Korea's new season is a disturbing reminder for Asians of global interconnectedness and the perils of environmental degradation.

5   "There is no way for us to deter this," said Kim Seung Bae, deputy director of South Korea's national weather service. "All we can do is try to forecast the yellow dust storms as early as possible, but with the current technology we can only detect it one day ahead of time at best. For now, our main innovation will be to add predictions of the intensity of the dust to our weather reports."

Photo: NASA image created by Jesse Allen, Earth Observatory, using data obtained from the MODIS Rapid Response team.

> **harmattan**
> a dry, dusty wind that blows along the northwest coast of Africa

6   In Seoul, a measurement of 70 **micrograms** of dust per cubic meter of air is considered normal during most of the year. At 1,000 micrograms, experts say, serious health warnings are indicated. Earlier this week, in the fourth storm of the season, a record measurement of 2,070 micrograms was reached in this city. Mr. Kim said two or three more storms could hit Korea this month.

7   Scientists say the dust storms, which are distinctly visible on regional satellite weather maps as gigantic yellow blobs, are the result of the rapid **desertification** in China and a prolonged drought affecting that country and other parts of Northeast Asia.

8   The term yellow dust refers to the color of the sand when it coats parked cars and windows rather than the color of the skies, which all this last week were a thick, acrid gray.

9   According to China's Environmental Protection Agency, the Gobi grew by 20,000 square miles from 1994 to 1999, and its steadily advancing edge now sits a mere 150 miles north of Beijing. As in West Africa, which weather experts say is the world's leading source of dust, China's environmental changes are accelerating because of overfarming, overgrazing and the widespread destruction of forests.

Gobi desert, China

> **micrograms**
> a unit of mass or weight equal to one millionth of a gram, used chiefly in microchemistry

China's Growing Deserts Are Suffocating Korea

10 But unlike West Africa's dust, which is carried to the southern United States by winds known as the tropical easterlies, dust from the Gobi and Taklimakan deserts in rapidly industrializing China is binding with toxic industrial pollutants, including arsenic, cadmium and lead, increasing the health threat.

Factory near Beijing, China

11 Changes like these have long made springtime synonymous with respiratory distress in Beijing. But as the dust storms have grown, their impact has been spreading rapidly eastward, blighting the air over the Korean peninsula and beyond. This has been an unusually dusty spring in Tokyo, for example, and fingerlike plumes of the airborne sand now travel 7,000 miles aboard the **jet stream** reaching Portland, Ore., and San Francisco, where the main effect so far has been to create breathtaking sunsets. "There is no smoking gun yet that proves that man is causing this," said Charles S. Zender, a professor of earth system science at the University of California at Irvine, "but rather lots of anecdotal evidence."

> **jet stream**
> *fast flowing, narrow air currents found in the atmospheres of some planets, including Earth*

Photo: © iStockphoto.com/Quan Long

12. "The puzzle of Asian dust is a huge question in weather science right now," he said, "and if human activity is proven to be the cause, it stands to reason that this problem is going to keep getting worse."

13. As a mood of resignation has set in over the persistence of this phenomenon, Koreans have already begun to focus on the economic costs. What was only recently regarded here as a minor nuisance is now seen as posing a serious threat in areas as diverse as public health, travel, retail shopping and even high-tech manufacturing.

14. This last week, for example, in addition to the school closures, scores of domestic flights have been canceled because of poor visibility. Workplace absenteeism has risen, too, and retail sales have dipped, as a result of people staying indoors.

15. "I've had a little bit of a cough," said Choi Byoung Su, 30, a businessman who was at a downtown pharmacy stocking up on medicine for a sore throat, which he said was caused by the dust storms. "I'm not too concerned about my health for now, but it is really a hassle for my car," he said, explaining that he needed to have it washed at least once a day now.

Air pollution in Beijing

Photo: © iStockphoto.com/Dave Logan

Dust Storms Graphic Organizer

Create a graphic organizer comparing the dust storms from the Dust Bowl in the 1930s and those affecting China and Korea today. You can use a T-chart, Venn diagram, or some other construction to organize your ideas.

Reading Passage for Lesson 25

Blizzard of 1966

By WTVH Channel 5 News Anchor, Ron Curtis, Syracuse, NY

1. It was all you could see—snow everywhere. Now, the warning for heavy snow went out Saturday, January 29th but nobody, nobody was prepared for the more than 3½ feet that fell over a 37-hour period. And it was piled even deeper in Oswego.

2. Eight and a half feet—think about that—8½ feet of snow! Well, they used helicopters to get badly needed supplies like food and coal to some isolated areas, and the weight of the snow also proved to be too much for some buildings.

The Blizzard of '66 and Lake Effect Snow

This storm is not so much known for it's blizzard conditions, which produced a foot of snow at Albany on the 29th and 30th, but for the intense lake **squalls** that developed as arctic air streamed across Lake Ontario on the 30th and 31st.

The Great Lakes **lee shore** effect combined with the cyclonic circulation to give an almost unbelievable 5-day total of 101 in. of snow at Oswego, N.Y. It is called **lake effect snow** and it occurs when cold winter winds pass over large expanses of warmer water. The warm moist air above the water wants to rise and, as it does, it eventually cools, releases water vapor, freezes and then dumps snow on the leeward shores.

lee shore
the shoreline away from the wind

Art: Copyright © Pearson Education, Inc., or its affiliates.
Photo: © iStockphoto.com/Grigoriy Likhatskiy

FOUNDATIONS • EXTREME WEATHER—LEVEL D | 149

Blizzard of 1966

reminisced
recalled the past

3   I also remember that many of us were snowed in here. We were put up at a nearby motel, but they started running out of food in a few days. And the final day that we were there when we went to the dining room for breakfast, we were told they'd run out of eggs, bacon, ham, bread, milk. So we asked if they had anything at all. And they said yes, they had prime rib. So that was our breakfast that day.

4   Schools were closed for about a week, and it was four or five days before most streets in the city were passable. And up north, bulldozers were used to clear the way for police and ambulance crews.

5   One of the local leaders charged with handling the emergency was then Onondaga county executive John Mulroy, who **reminisced** about the storm and its aftermath:

> "The intensity and the very widespread coverage of that particular storm caught everybody by surprise. And it turned out to be a disaster."

6   John Mulroy was Onondaga county's first county executive, and he was at the helm when the blizzard of '66 hit. Twenty-seven years later, Mulroy watched from the sidelines as county and city officials coped with a storm with far more resources at their disposal than he and Syracuse mayor Bill Walsh had available.

7   "People didn't have snowmobiles in those days, and they didn't have 4-wheel drive vehicles, and it was a much slower process getting out. I remember there were city streets, even, that weren't open for a week. One street had 20 feet of snow in it. The only way to get rid of it was to pick it up and carry it away, which we did."

8   Mulroy still remembers how many county and city employees somehow managed to get to their jobs and how others stayed at their posts for days when their relief couldn't get in—another example of community spirit at its finest.

Video for Lesson 25

Blizzard of 1966

Report	Location	How the Images and Comments Connect to Ron's Narrative
1		
2		
3		
4		

Photo: © iStockphoto.com/Chad Truemper

FOUNDATIONS • EXTREME WEATHER—LEVEL D

Blizzards—1966 and Today

Discuss how Ron's story might change if, in 1966, people had all the same tools and technologies that we use today.

Reading Passage for Lessons 26–27

Winter Storms
The Deceptive Killers

A snow storm blankets the mid-Atlantic states with snow.

deceptive
perceptually misleading

1. This preparedness guide explains the dangers of winter weather and suggests life-saving action you can take. With this information, you can recognize winter weather threats, develop an action plan and be ready when severe winter weather threatens. Remember… your safety is up to you.

Why Talk about Winter Weather?

2. - Each year, dozens of Americans die due to **exposure** to cold. Add to that number, vehicle accidents and fatalities, fires due to dangerous use of heaters and other winter weather fatalities and you have a significant threat.

Photo: NASA Earth Observatory image created by Jesse Allen, using data provided courtesy of the MODIS Rapid Response team

Winter Storms

utilities
public services, such as a telephone or electric-light system, a streetcar or railroad line, or the like

- Threats such as hypothermia and frostbite can lead to loss of fingers and toes or cause permanent kidney, pancreas, liver injury, and even death. You must prepare properly to avoid these extreme dangers. You also need to know what to do if you see symptoms of these threats.

- A major winter storm can last for several days and be accompanied by high winds, freezing rain or sleet, heavy snowfall, and cold temperatures.

- People can become trapped at home or in a car, without **utilities** or other assistance.

- Attempting to walk for help in a winter storm can be a deadly decision.

- The aftermath of a winter storm can have an impact on a community or region for days, weeks, or even months.

- Extremely cold temperatures, heavy snow, and coastal flooding can cause hazardous conditions and hidden problems.

Heavy snowstorm in Massachusetts

Photo: © iStockphoto.com/Denis Tangney Jr.

Dangerous driving in a snowstorm

Heavy Snow

3. Heavy snow can **immobilize** a region and paralyze a city, stranding commuters, closing airports, stopping the flow of supplies, and disrupting emergency and medical services. **Accumulations** of snow can cause roofs to collapse and knock down trees and power lines. Homes and farms may be isolated for days and unprotected livestock may be lost. In the mountains, heavy snow can lead to avalanches. The cost of snow removal, repairing damages, and the loss of business can have severe economic impacts on cities and towns. An avalanche is a mass of tumbling snow. More than 80 percent of midwinter avalanches are triggered by a rapid accumulation of snow, and 90 percent of those occur within 24 hours of snowfall. An avalanche may reach a mass of a million tons and travel at speeds up to 200 mph.

4. **Blizzard:** Winds of 35 mph or more with snow and blowing snow reducing **visibility** to less than ¼ mile for 3 hours or more.

Blowing snow: Wind-driven snow that reduces visibility. Blowing snow may be falling snow and/or snow on the ground picked up by the wind.

Photo: © iStockphoto.com/Bill Grove

immobilize
to prevent the use, activity, or movement of

visibility
the relative ability to be seen under given conditions of distance, light, atmosphere

Winter Storms

Snow squalls: Brief, intense snow showers accompanied by strong, gusty winds. Accumulation may be significant.

Snow showers: Snow falling at varying intensities for brief periods of time. Some accumulation is possible.

Snow flurries: Light snow falling for short durations with little or no accumulation.

Ice

5   Heavy accumulations of ice can bring down trees and topple utility poles and communication towers. Ice can disrupt communications and power for days while utility companies repair extensive damage. Even small accumulations of ice can be extremely dangerous to motorists and pedestrians. Bridges and overpasses are particularly dangerous because they freeze before other surfaces.

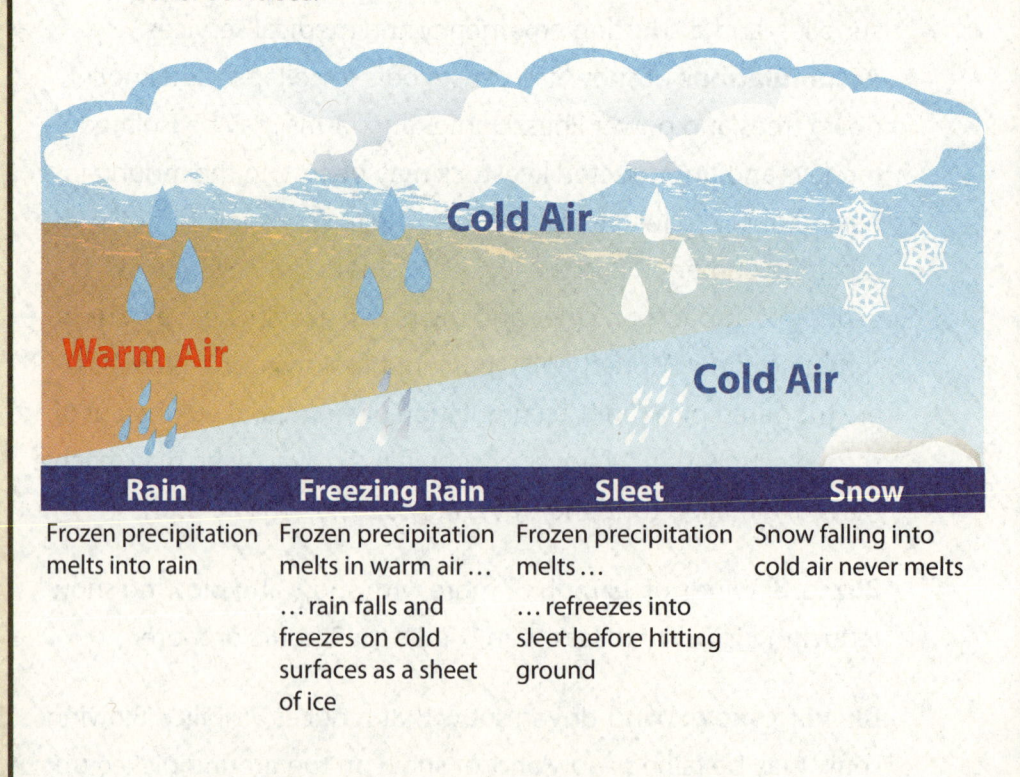

Rain	Freezing Rain	Sleet	Snow
Frozen precipitation melts into rain	Frozen precipitation melts in warm air … … rain falls and freezes on cold surfaces as a sheet of ice	Frozen precipitation melts … … refreezes into sleet before hitting ground	Snow falling into cold air never melts

Art: Copyright © Pearson Education, Inc., or its affiliates, adapted from NOAA.

Power lines brought down by ice

Winter Flooding

6 Winter storms can generate coastal flooding, ice jams and snow melt, resulting in significant damage and loss of life.

Coastal floods: Winds generated from intense winter storms can cause widespread tidal flooding and severe beach erosion along coastal areas.

Ice jams: Long cold spells can cause rivers and lakes to freeze. A rise in the water level or a thaw breaks the ice into large chunks, which become jammed at man made and natural **obstructions**. Ice jams can act as a dam, resulting in severe flooding.

Snow melt: Sudden thaw of a heavy snow pack often leads to flooding.

> **obstructions**
> *things that block your path, hindrances*

Winter Storms

Cold

7 Exposure to cold can cause frostbite or hypothermia and become life-threatening. Infants and elderly people are most susceptible. What constitutes extreme cold varies in different parts of the country. In the South, near freezing temperatures are considered extreme cold. Freezing temperatures can cause severe damage to citrus fruit crops and other vegetation. Pipes may freeze and burst in homes that are poorly insulated or without heat. In the North, extreme cold means temperatures well below zero.

8 **Wind chill** is not the actual temperature but rather how wind and cold feel on exposed skin. As the wind increases, heat is carried away from the body at an accelerated rate, driving down the body temperature. Animals are also affected by wind chill; however, cars, plants and other objects are not.

9 **Frostbite** is damage to body tissue caused by extreme cold. A wind chill of -20° Fahrenheit (F) will cause frostbite in just 30 minutes. Frostbite causes a loss of feeling and a white or pale appearance in extremities, such as fingers, toes, ear lobes or the tip of the nose. If symptoms are detected, get medical help immediately! If you must wait for help, slowly rewarm affected areas. However, if the person is also showing signs of hypothermia, warm the body core before the extremities.

10 **Hypothermia** is a condition brought on when the body temperature drops to less than 95°F. It can kill. For those who survive, there are likely to be lasting kidney, liver and pancreas problems. Warning signs include uncontrollable shivering, memory loss, disorientation, incoherence, slurred speech, drowsiness and apparent exhaustion. Take the person's temperature. If below 95°F, seek medical care immediately!

11. **If medical care is not available,** warm the person slowly, starting with the body core. Warming the arms and legs first drives cold blood toward the heart and can lead to heart failure. If necessary, use your body heat to help. Get the person into dry clothing and wrap in a warm blanket covering the head and neck. Do not give the person alcohol, drugs, coffee or any hot beverage or food. Warm broth is the first food to offer.

Winter Storm Hazards in the U.S.
Annual Mean Snowfall

Alaska
- Heavy snow
- Strong winds/Blizzards
- Coastal flooding
- Extreme cold
- Avalanches
- Ice jams
- Ice fog

The West Coast
- Heavy precipitation
- High winds
- Coastal flooding
- Beach erosion

The Rockies
- Heavy snow
- Mountain-effect snow
- Strong winds
- Avalanches
- Extreme cold
- Blizzards

Midwest and Plains
- Heavy snow
- Strong winds/Blizzards
- Extreme wind chill
- Lake-effect snow
- Ice storms

Mid-Atlantic to New England
- Heavy snow
- Ice storms
- Strong winds
- Coastal flooding
- Beach erosion
- Extreme cold

Southeast and Gulf Coast
- Ice storms
- Crop-killing freezes
- Occasional snow

Inches
- 0.0
- 0.1 - 3.0
- 3.1 - 6.0
- 6.1 - 12.0
- 12.1 - 24.0
- 24.1 - 36.0
- 36.1 - 48.0
- 48.1 - 72.0
- > 72.0

Photo: © iStockphoto.com/Оксана Ткачук
Art: NOAA

Winter Storms

How Winter Storms Form

12 There are many ways for winter storms to form; however, all have three key components.

Cold Air: For snow and ice to form, the temperature must be below freezing in the clouds and near the ground.

Moisture: Water evaporating from bodies of water, such as a large lake or the ocean, is an excellent source of moisture.

Lift: Lift causes moisture to rise and form clouds and precipitation. An example of lift is warm air colliding with cold air and being forced to rise. Another example of lift is air flowing up a mountain side.

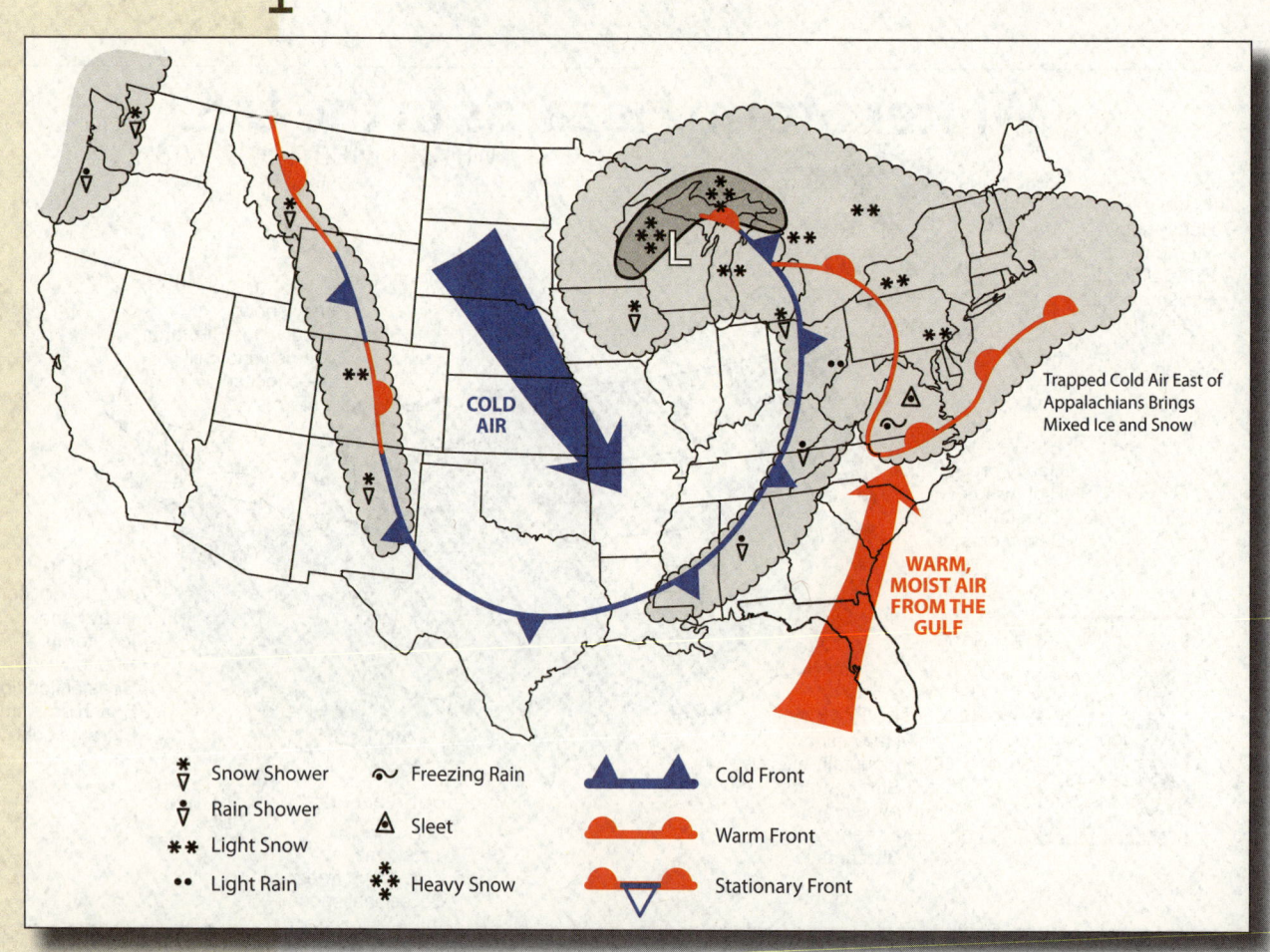

Trapped Cold Air East of Appalachians Brings Mixed Ice and Snow

COLD AIR

WARM, MOIST AIR FROM THE GULF

Symbol		Symbol		Symbol	
Snow Shower		Freezing Rain		Cold Front	
Rain Shower		Sleet		Warm Front	
Light Snow		Heavy Snow		Stationary Front	
Light Rain					

Art: Copyright © Pearson Education, Inc., or its affiliates, adapted from NOAA.

Warm Front
warm air
cold air

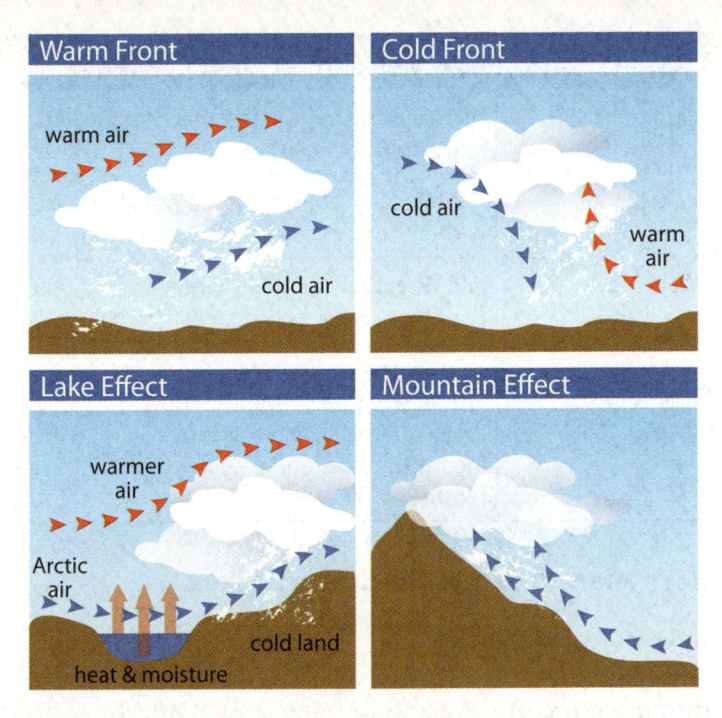

Cold Front
cold air
warm air

Lake Effect
warmer air
Arctic air
cold land
heat & moisture

Mountain Effect

NOAA Weather Radio—the best way to receive warnings from the National Weather Service

13 The National Weather Service continuously broadcasts warnings and forecasts that can be received by NOAA Weather Radios, which are sold in many stores. The average range is 40 miles, depending on topography. Purchase a radio that has a battery back-up and a Specific Area Message Encoder feature, which automatically alerts you when a watch or warning is issued for your county or parish.

What to Listen For

14 The National Weather Service issues outlooks, watches, warnings and advisories for all winter weather hazards. Here's what they mean and what to do. Use the information below to make an informed decision on your risk and what actions should be taken. Remember to listen to your local officials' recommendations and to NOAA Weather Radio for the latest winter storm information.

Art: Copyright © Pearson Education, Inc., or its affiliates, adapted from NOAA.
Photo: © iStockphoto.com/Murat Giray Kaya

Winter Storms

15

NWS issued…	What it is…	What to do…
Outlook	Winter storm conditions are possible in the next 2–5 days.	Stay tuned to local media for updates.
Watch	Winter storm conditions are possible within the next 36–48 hours.	Prepare now!
Warning	Life-threatening severe winter conditions have begun or will begin within 24 hours.	Act now!
Advisory	Winter weather conditions are expected to cause significant inconveniences and may be hazardous.	If you are cautious, these situations should not be life threatening.

Be Prepared! Before the Storm Strikes

At Home and Work

16 Primary concerns are loss of heat, power and telephone service, and a shortage of supplies if storm conditions continue for more than a day. Check the list for what to have on hand.

- Flashlight and extra batteries.

- Battery-powered NOAA Weather Radio and portable radio to receive emergency information. These may be your only links to the outside.

- Extra food and water. Have high energy food, such as dried fruit, nuts and granola bars, and food requiring no cooking or refrigeration.

- Extra medicine and baby items.

- First-aid supplies, including heating fuel. Refuel before you are empty. Fuel carriers may not reach you for days after a winter storm.

Photo: © iStockphoto.com/Dana Bartekoske

- Emergency heat source: fireplace, wood stove, space heater. Use properly and ventilate to prevent a fire.

- Fire extinguisher and smoke alarm. Test smoke alarms once a month to ensure they work properly.

- Make sure pets have plenty of food, water and shelter.

In Vehicles

17. Plan your travel and check the latest weather reports to avoid the storm! Fully check and winterize your vehicle before the winter season begins. Carry a Winter Storm Survival Kit:

- Mobile phone, charger, batteries
- Blankets/sleeping bags
- Flashlight with extra batteries
- First-aid kit
- Knife
- High-calorie, non-perishable food
- Extra clothing to keep dry
- Large empty can to use as emergency toilet. Tissues and paper towels for sanitary purposes

- Small can and waterproof matches to melt snow for drinking water
- Sack of sand or cat litter for traction
- Shovel
- Windshield scraper and brush
- Tool kit
- Tow rope
- Battery booster cables
- Water container
- Compass and road maps.

Photo: © iStockphoto.com/Ionescu Bogdan Cristian

Winter Storms

Keep your gas tank near full to avoid ice in the tank and fuel lines. Avoid traveling alone. Let someone know your timetable and primary and alternate routes.

On the Farm/Pets

18 Move animals to sheltered areas. Shelter belts, properly laid out and oriented, are better protection for cattle than confining shelters, such as sheds. Haul extra feed to nearby feeding areas. Have water available. Most animals die from dehydration in winter storms. Make sure pets have plenty of food, water and shelter.

When Caught in a Winter Storm

Outside

19 <u>Find shelter</u>
Try to stay dry. Cover all exposed body parts.

<u>No shelter?</u>
Build a lean-to, a windbreak or a snow cave for protection from the wind. Build a fire for heat and to attract attention. Place rocks around the fire to absorb and reflect heat. Melt snow for drinking water. Eating snow will lower your body temperature.

Photo: © iStockphoto.com/Robert Koopmans

Lessons 26–27

In a Vehicle

20 Stay in vehicle
You will become quickly disoriented in wind-driven snow and cold. Run the motor about 10 minutes each hour for heat. Open the window a little for fresh air to avoid carbon monoxide poisoning. Make sure the exhaust pipe is not blocked.

Be visible to rescuers
Turn on the dome light at night when running the engine. Tie a colored cloth, preferably red, to your antenna or door. After snow stops falling, raise the hood to indicate you need help.

Exercise
From time to time, move arms, legs, fingers and toes vigorously to keep blood circulating and to keep warm.

Photo: © iStockphoto.com/Ziga Lisjak

Winter Storms

Inside

21 <u>Stay inside</u>
When using alternate heat from a fireplace, wood stove, space heater, etc., use fire safeguards and properly ventilate.

<u>No heat?</u>
Close off unneeded rooms. Stuff towels or rags in cracks under doors. Cover windows at night. Eat and drink. Food provides the body with energy for producing its own heat. Keep the body replenished with fluids to prevent dehydration. Wear layers of loose-fitting, lightweight, warm clothing. Remove layers to avoid overheating, perspiration and **subsequent** chill.

> **subsequent**
> occurring or coming later or after

Photos: © iStockphoto.com/Alexey Stiop (top); © iStockphoto.com/Артем Устинов (bottom)

Family Disaster Plan

22 Prepare for hazards that affect your area with a Family Disaster Plan. Where will your family be when disaster strikes? They could be anywhere at work, at school or in the car. How will you find each other? Will you know if your children are safe? Disasters may force you to evacuate your neighborhood or confine you to your home. What would you do if basic services—water, gas, electricity or telephones—were cut off?

Steps to Take

23 **Gather information about hazards:** Contact your local National Weather Service office, emergency management office, and American Red Cross chapter. Find out what type of disasters could occur and how you should respond. Learn your community's warning signals and evacuation plans. Assess your risks and identify ways to make your home and property more secure.

24 **Meet with your family to create a plan:** Discuss your plan with your family. Pick two places to meet: a spot outside your home for an emergency such as a fire, and a place away from your neighborhood in case you can't return home. Choose an out-of-state friend as your "family check-in contact" for everyone to call if the family gets separated. Discuss what you would do if advised to evacuate.

Photo: © iStockphoto.com/Ekaterina Minaeva

Winter Storms

25 **Implement your plan:**

1. Post emergency telephone numbers by the phone.

2. Install safety features in your home, such as smoke alarms and fire extinguishers.

3. Inspect your home for potential hazards (items that can move, fall, break or catch fire) and correct them.

4. Have your family learn basic safety measures. These include CPR, AED and basic first aid; operation of a fire extinguisher; and knowing how and when to turn off water, gas and electricity in the home.

5. Teach children how and when to call 911 or your local Emergency Medical Services number.

6. Keep enough supplies in your home for at least three days. Assemble a disaster supplies kit. Store these supplies in sturdy, easy-to-carry containers, such as backpacks or duffle bags. Keep important documents in a waterproof container. Keep a smaller disaster supplies kit in the trunk of your car.

Photo: © iStockphoto.com/Richard Goerg

Winter Storm Hazards

Find where you live (or would like to live) on the "Winter Storm Hazards in the U.S." map. What winter hazards might you face? Have you ever faced them? If so, what did you do? What do you think you or your family could do to prepare for the winter hazards in your area?

_____
_____
_____
_____
_____
_____
_____
_____
_____
_____
_____
_____
_____
_____
_____
_____
_____
_____
_____

Being Prepared

Choose one of the disasters discussed in class that could affect your area. Write a paragraph describing what you and your family could do to prepare for the disaster.

Reading Passage for Lessons 28–29

Climate Change Basics

Photo: NASA

The Greenhouse Effect

1. The Earth's atmosphere, a layer of gases and microscopic dust that surrounds the planet, acts like a greenhouse in keeping the Earth warm enough to support life. Like the glass panes in a greenhouse, gases in the atmosphere let sunlight pass through and warm Earth's surface, and limit the amount of heat that escapes back into space. Without this greenhouse effect, the Earth would be a frozen planet.

2. Energy emitted from the sun, known as solar radiation, which includes visible light, infrared radiation and ultraviolet radiation, passes through the atmosphere and is either absorbed or reflected back from clouds or the earth's surface. Darker surfaces like vegetation and asphalt absorb more energy than lighter surfaces like ice and snow. This process warms the planet's land and water surfaces.

FOUNDATIONS • EXTREME WEATHER—LEVEL D | 171

Climate Change Basics

Figure 1

The Greenhouse Effect

Solar radiation passes through the clear atmosphere.

Some solar radiation is reflected by the Earth and the atmosphere.

Some of the infrared radiation passes through the atmosphere, and some is absorbed and re-emitted in all directions by greenhouse gas molecules. The effect of this is to warm the Earth's surface and the lower atmosphere.

Most radiation is absorbed by the Earth's surface and warms it.

Infrared radiation is emitted from the Earth's surface.

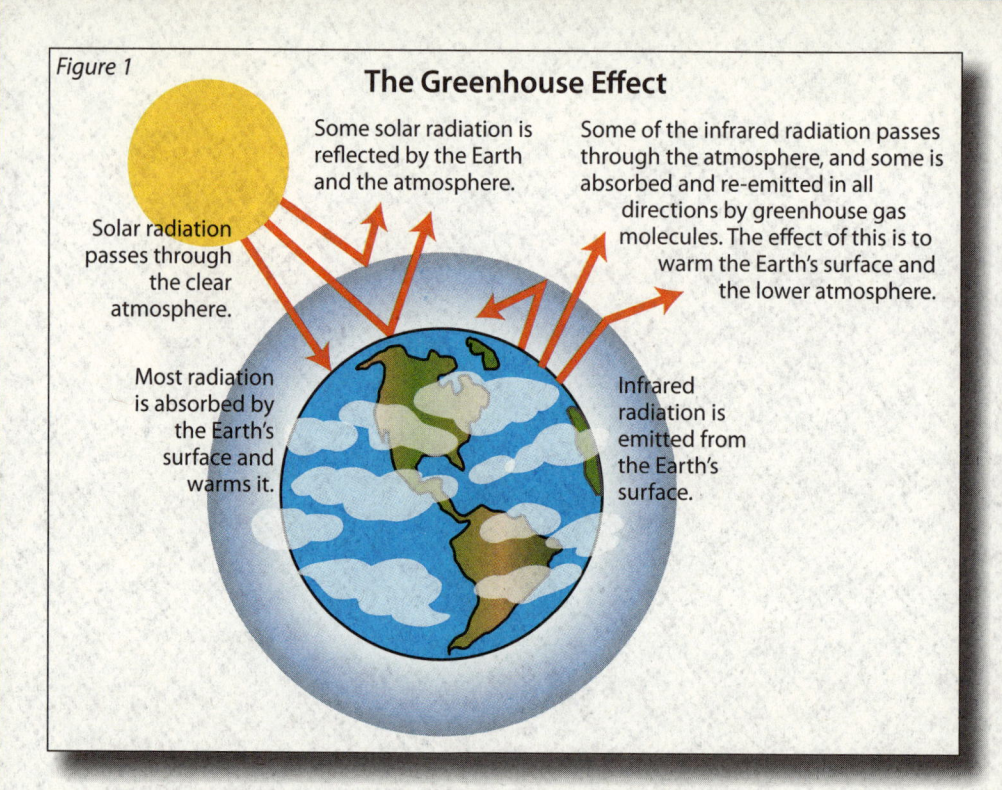

3   The Earth's surface warms the air above it by radiating its energy as infrared radiation. Some of this infrared radiation escapes out to space, while some remains trapped in the atmosphere by **greenhouse gases**. Naturally occurring greenhouse gases, like water vapor and carbon dioxide, absorb the heat, keeping the planet warm enough for life to survive.

Climate Change and the Human Connection

4   Greenhouse gases occur naturally in our environment and serve a critical role in keeping our planet livable. However, greenhouses gases are also emitted from man-made sources. The burning of fossil fuels such as coal and oil emits carbon dioxide, the most common greenhouse gas. Since the Industrial Revolution, as energy needs have grown in our society, the rate of greenhouse gases emitted into the atmosphere has been increasing. The atmosphere's over abundance of greenhouse gases is enhancing the Earth's greenhouse effect, leading to warmer temperatures and changes in climate around the planet.

Art: Copyright © Pearson Education, Inc., or its affiliates.

A coal power plant

Climate and Weather

Heat Makes It All Happen

5   Weather is driven by heat, the rotation of the Earth, and variations in the Earth's surface. Heat from the sun warms the Earth's land and oceans, which in turn heat the air above their surface. The warm air then rises and is replaced by neighboring cooler air. This movement creates currents of air that distribute heat across the planet. Ocean currents also distribute heat around the planet. As heated air and water move around the Earth and mix with colder air and water, we get weather in the form of clouds, rain, and wind. Other factors, like how much sunlight hits a region, nearby bodies of water, and how flat or mountainous an area is, affect weather conditions around the globe. For instance, a mountain range could stop rain clouds from passing through. As a result, one side of the mountain will be lush with forests while the other side may be dry.

Climate Change Basics

6   Climate describes weather patterns in an area over a long period of time, 30 years or more. Earth's climate has changed over the planet's five billion year history through different ice ages and warming periods. However, these climate changes occurred over periods of thousands of years.

Climate Change and the Human Connection

7   The Earth's average temperature has increased by one degree Fahrenheit over the past 100 years. Scientists have recorded an overall global warming trend, with the most rapid warming occurring over the last twenty years. Scientists believe that the increasing concentration of greenhouse gases in Earth's atmosphere is affecting global temperatures by enhancing the planet's greenhouse effect. The warming of the atmosphere is currently affecting, and will continue to affect, weather conditions around the planet. Expected weather impacts include changes to rainfall patterns; more frequent and intense droughts and flashfloods; and less snowfall in mountain ranges.

Drought-affected farm land

Photo: © iStockphoto.com/Brandon Jennings

Air Pollution

8   Air pollution is comprised of gases and particles emitted in the air that can be harmful to human health and the environment. Some air pollution may be caused by natural events like forest fires and volcano eruptions; however, most air pollution comes from man-made sources. The biggest source of air pollution is from the burning of fossil fuels, such as coal and oil for energy in transportation, power plants, and factories. Some of the more prevalent forms of man-made pollution include smog, particulate matter, and greenhouse gases.

9   The main component of smog is ozone (O_3), a colorless gas. Exposure to ozone can trigger chest pain, coughing, throat irritation, and can cause respiratory diseases. Harmful concentrations of ozone occur when pollutants we call nitrogen oxides (NO and NO_2) and volatile organic compounds (VOCs) react in sunlight to form ozone. Nitrogen oxides and VOCs are emitted by vehicle exhaust, gasoline vapors, industrial emissions, and even consumer products. Many urban areas experience unhealthy levels of ozone in the summertime. However, less urban areas may also experience high ozone levels because wind can carry nitrogen oxides, VOCs, and even ozone miles away from their original sources. In some cases, mountains can stop the transport of pollutants, resulting in extremely harmful ozone concentrations in areas like Los Angeles in California.

The Los Angeles skyline hidden by smog

Photo: © iStockphoto.com/Ana Abejon

10. Particulate matter (PM) is composed of tiny particles and liquid droplets. It is made up of various components, such as acids, organic chemicals, metals, and dust particles. These small particles can lodge into the lungs and even invade the bloodstream. The most dangerous particles are the smallest: those less than 10 micrometers in diameter, such as those found near roadways and dusty industries; and fine particles less than 2.5 micrometers in diameter, such as those found in smoke and haze. Breathing in PM can result in serious health effects, like respiratory diseases, irregular heartbeat, and premature death in people with heart or lung disease. PM is emitted from diesel exhaust, industrial processes, and construction activities. In the wintertime, wood burning in fireplaces is often the biggest source of PM.

Wood-burning fireplaces are a large source of particulate matter.

Climate Change

11. Among the most emitted man-made greenhouse gases is carbon dioxide (CO_2). CO_2 occurs naturally but is also emitted from the burning of fossil fuels. The amount of CO_2 in the atmosphere has been increasing significantly as fossil fuel use has grown around the world. While CO_2 emissions do not usually cause immediate health impacts, they accumulate in the atmosphere for hundreds of years and contribute to climate change. In 1970, the United States passed the Clean Air Act to control air pollution and protect human health and the environment. As part of the Act, the Environmental Protection Agency set limits for major pollutants, including ozone, NO_2 and PM. States are required to meet these limits by regulating and reducing air pollution emissions in their state.

12   Since smog formation is directly related to warm days, air quality is expected to worsen as temperatures increase from global warming. Higher temperatures and more smog threaten public health with more respiratory and heat related illnesses. In addition, climate change is expected to increase fire hazards contributing to higher levels of air pollution.

The Carbon Cycle

13   Carbon is a key element in all living matter, found in people, animals, soil, and oceans. Trees, plants, and fossil fuels store carbon. Carbon circulates through Earth's environment, moving between the atmosphere, trees, plants, animals, people, land, and water. Carbon exists in the atmosphere as carbon dioxide, a greenhouse gas.

14   Trees and plants use sunlight, water, and carbon dioxide to make food through photosynthesis. Carbon is then stored in trees and plants until they are eaten, burned, or decomposed. Animals consume the carbon in plants and release carbon dioxide through respiration. When burned, plants and trees release their stored carbon into the atmosphere as carbon dioxide.

15   As plants and trees decompose, their stored carbon breaks down into the soil and can even turn into a fossil fuel after thousand of years of compression. Once the fossil fuel is burned the stored carbon is emitted as carbon dioxide. Carbon dioxide is absorbed from the atmosphere by plants and trees for food. Oceans also absorb carbon dioxide.

16   People are emitting carbon dioxide into the air faster than the planet is absorbing it, leading to an accumulation of carbon dioxide in the atmosphere. The surplus of carbon dioxide in the atmosphere is enhancing the planet's greenhouse effect, leading to global warming and climate change.

Climate Change Basics

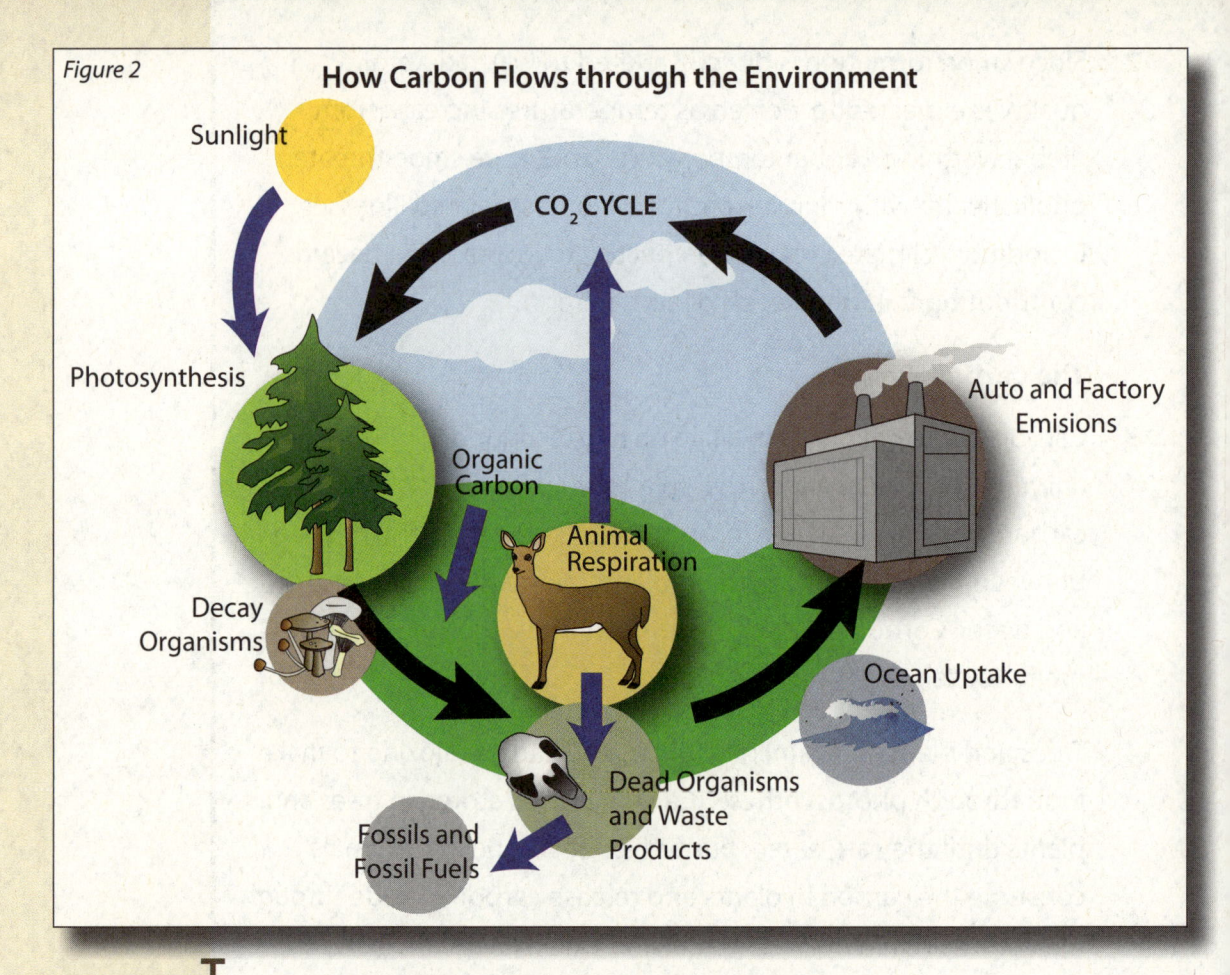

Figure 2

How Carbon Flows through the Environment

- Sunlight
- Photosynthesis
- CO₂ CYCLE
- Organic Carbon
- Animal Respiration
- Auto and Factory Emisions
- Decay Organisms
- Ocean Uptake
- Fossils and Fossil Fuels
- Dead Organisms and Waste Products

Climate Change Impacts and Causes

17 Climate change refers to the changes in climate that are occurring, and are expected to occur, due to the warming of the planet. Small shifts in climate are already being seen around the world with the melting of glaciers and changing weather conditions. In California, the climate is expected to become considerably warmer. It is impossible to predict the exact degree to which temperature will change, but the extent of change will depend on individual actions, as well as the decisions societies and governments make in the next several years.

18 Scientists predict that a medium warming scenario of 5 to 8 degrees Fahrenheit by 2090 would significantly reduce the snow pack in the Sierra Nevada, raise sea levels, and lead to more

Art: Copyright © Pearson Education, Inc., or its affiliates.

The Sierra Nevada snow pack could be greatly reduced by climate change.

heat waves, wildfires, and air pollution. The possibility of such climate changes threaten human health, agriculture, natural resources, coastal landforms and communities, and plant and animal habitats, to name only a few. For example, reduced snow pack means that there will be less water available for agriculture and irrigation of croplands, for drinking, and for hydropower generation.

Global Reach of Volcanic Gases

19. When we think of the negative impact that volcanoes have on people, the local geographic area of the eruption generally comes to mind. Ash, lava, and mudflows are all destructive and hazardous for people who live close to volcanoes. A less well-known product of eruptions, however, sometimes has a more widespread effect. The gases emitted by volcanoes can, under certain circumstances, affect global climate and even cause mass extinctions of flora and fauna.

Climate Change Basics

20 Sulfur dioxide (SO_2) is the main gas released by volcanoes that can affect climate in the short term. Chemical reactions that occur when SO_2 reaches the atmosphere produce tiny sulfuric acid droplets called "aerosol." Very energetic eruptions push the aerosol up into the stratosphere, the layer of the atmosphere from 10 to 50 km altitude (around 32,000 to 164,000 ft), where it inhibits the sun's energy from reaching and warming the earth's surface. Once in the stratospheric jet stream, the aerosol quickly encircles the globe. The microscopic droplets tend to remain aloft for months to years, promoting global cooling.

21 In the longer term, huge volcanic eruptions can have another effect. The release of greenhouse gases, such as carbon dioxide, into the atmosphere can cause warming rather than cooling. Notable eruptions in recent years appear to have affected climate. One example is the 1991 eruption of Mount Pinatubo in the Philippines, which injected nearly 20 million tons of SO_2 into the stratosphere that became dispersed around the globe in about 3 weeks. The recorded effect was a 0.5 degrees C (0.9 degrees F) drop in temperature for the following two years. Remember, this small-sounding temperature decrease is a global average.

The June 12, 1991 eruption column from Mount Pinatubo taken from the east side of Clark Air Base in the Philippines. The release of ash and gases from volcanic eruptions such as this one can impact climate across the world.

Photo: USGS/Cascades Volcano Observatory/Dave Harlow

22   Even small temperature changes can affect weather systems. The year after the eruption, the U.S. experienced its third coldest and wettest summer in 77 years, and major flooding of the Mississippi River occurred. These observations are consistent with predictions made by climate modelers of Pinatubo's effect. The much larger eruption of Tambora, Indonesia, in 1815 produced the greatest volcanic effects on climate in recorded history, with as much as 1 degree C (1.8 degrees F) global temperature decrease, causing crop failures in Europe the following year, termed "the year without a summer."

Climate Change Connection

23   Governments and organizations around the world are working hard to reduce the greenhouse gas that are man-made emissions and protect the climate, however they need help. There is not much we can do to stop natural emissions like forest fires and volcanic gas, but we can cut back on the man-made air pollutants. Many of the choices individuals make every day at home, in schools, or in workplaces affect the amount of pollution that is emitted into the environment. Conserving energy; recycling cans, bottles, and paper; choosing non-toxic environmentally friendly products; walking more and driving less are all actions that reduce greenhouse gas emissions. If *all* individuals do their part there is a greater chance of protecting a healthy environment, healthy air quality, and a stable climate.

Human Connection to Climate Change

Write a paragraph explaining the human connection to climate change. Be sure to use evidence from the text to support your answer.

_____
_____
_____
_____
_____
_____
_____
_____
_____
_____
_____
_____
_____
_____
_____
_____
_____
_____
_____
_____

Climate and Societies

Answer the questions below. Use evidence from the text to support your answers.

1. With all this new information on climates, how do climates shape our societies?

   _____
   _____
   _____
   _____
   _____
   _____

2. How do we model our lives around the climate we live in?

   _____
   _____
   _____
   _____
   _____
   _____

3. What are the effects on society if they do not take the climate into consideration?

   _____
   _____
   _____
   _____
   _____
   _____
   _____
   _____

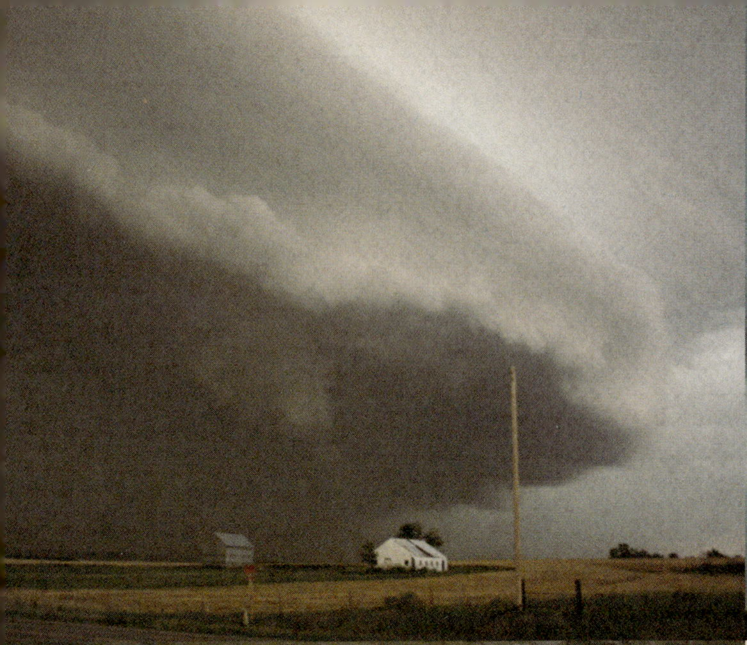
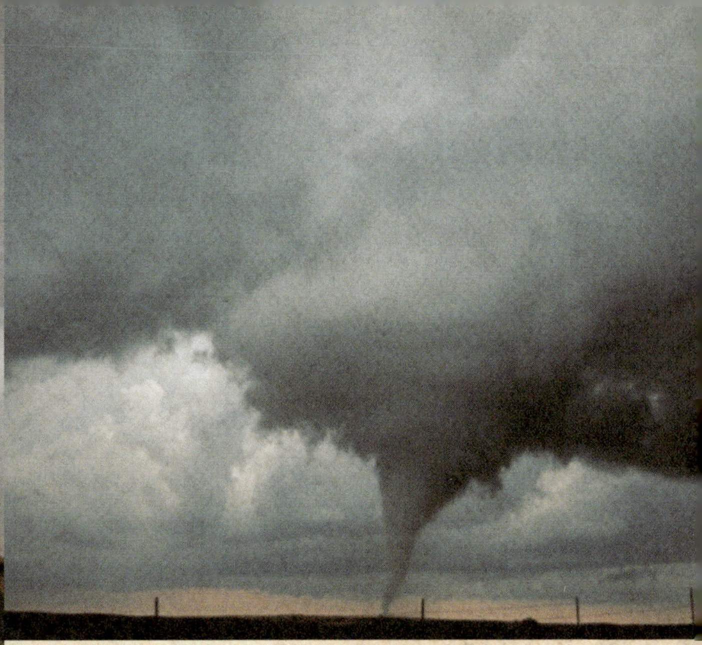
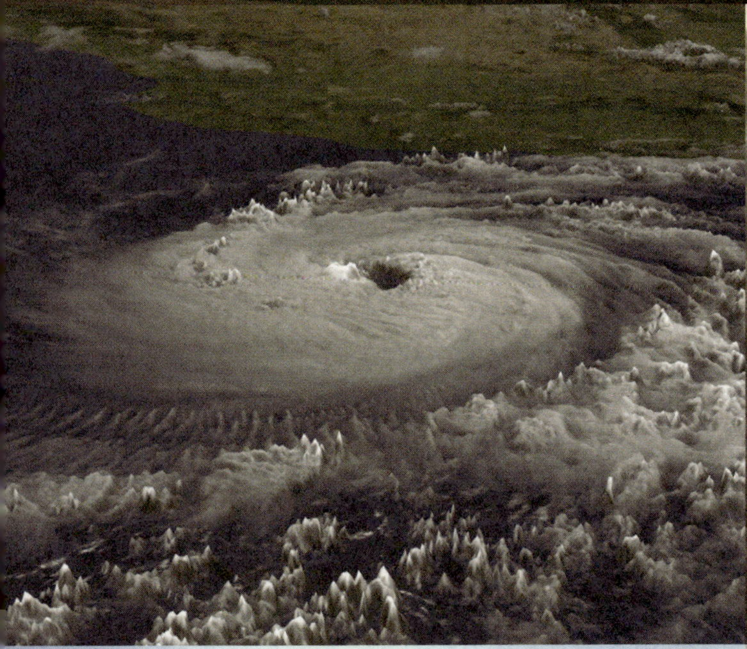
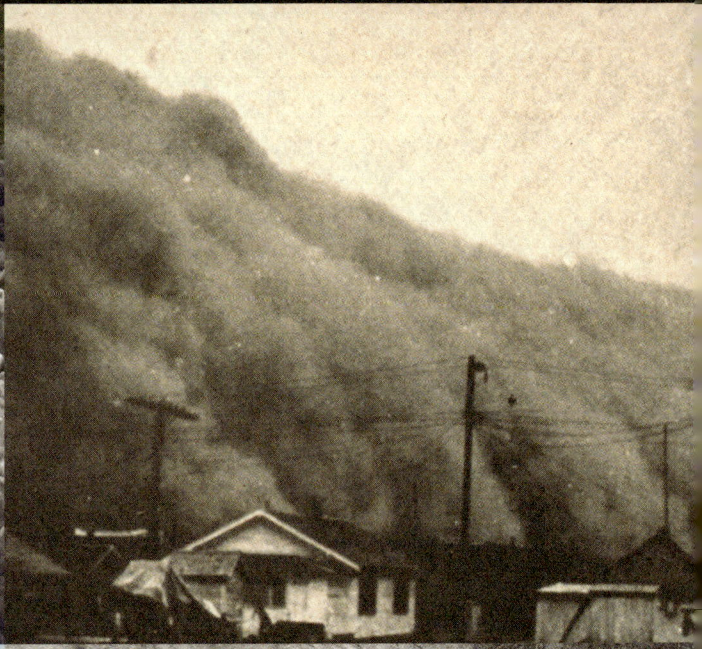
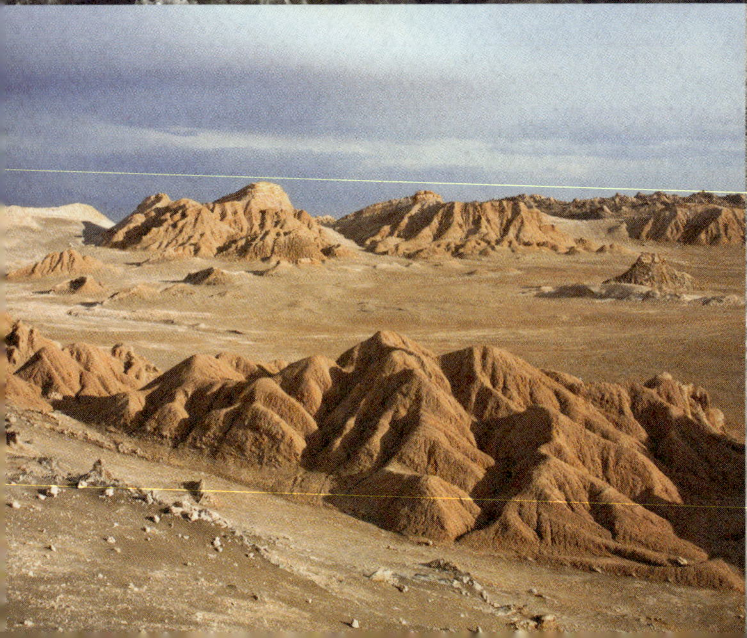
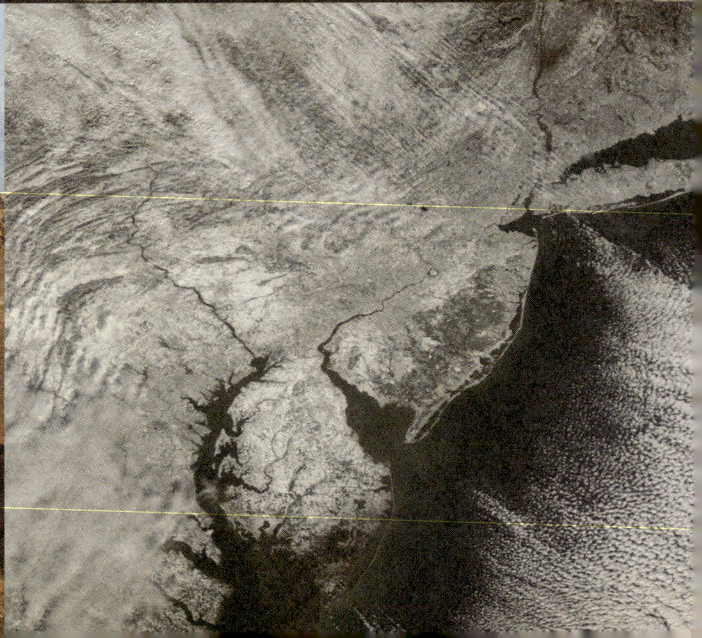

Lesson 30

Culminating Project

Natural Disasters, Extreme Weather Culminating Project

- My extreme weather project should:
  - Explain the affects of extreme weather on humans and our society or the affects of humans on extreme weather.
  - Present accurate information.
  - Be well organized.
  - Be easy to read and understand.
  - Present an argument using three to five sources.

Research Project

You will conduct a short research project that argues one side of the issue of whether extreme weather affects humans or humans affect extreme weather using three to five sources of information about extreme weather from the module or another resource such as the Internet or books. Your project will include both a written and oral component. First, you will write your argument in support of your stance and then present your argument to your peers.

Required Pieces of an Argument

- Introduce a claim, acknowledge alternate or opposing claims, and organize the reasons and evidence logically.
- Support the claim with logical reasoning and relevant evidence, using accurate, credible sources and demonstrating an understanding of the topic.
- Use words, phrases, and clauses to create cohesion and clarify the relationships among the claim, reasons, and evidence.
- Establish and maintain a formal style.
- Provide a concluding statement that follows from and supports the argument presented.

Photos, opposite page, left to right, starting at top: Sean Waugh NOAA/NSSL; OAR/ERL/National Severe Storms Laboratory (NSSL); NOAA; NOAA, NOAA's National Weather Service (NWS) Collection; © iStockphoto.com/José Carlos Pires Pereira; NASA Earth Observatory image created by Jesse Allen, using data provided courtesy of the MODIS Rapid Response team

Project Planning Sheet

Stance: _____

Point 1: _____
_____
_____

Source for point 1: _____

Point 2: _____
_____
_____

Source for point 2: _____

Point 3: _____
_____
_____

Source for point 3: _____

Point 4: _____
_____
_____

Source for point 4: _____

Point 5: _____
_____
_____

Source for point 5: _____

Argument Rubric for Culminating Project

Directions: Use this rubric as a guide as you write your argument. A good argument will have all these elements.

Criteria	4	3	2	1
Introduces a claim	The opening introduces a claim clearly and in an especially unique and engaging way and acknowledges alternate or opposing claims.	The opening introduces a claim and acknowledges alternate or opposing claims.	The opening introduces a claim in an unclear manner or fails to acknowledge other claims.	The opening does not introduce a claim.
Organizes the reasons and evidence logically	The piece organizes the reasons and evidence clearly and logically.	The piece organizes the reasons and evidence logically.	The piece organizes the reasons and evidence, but not always in a logical manner.	The piece does not organize reasons and evidence logically or they are missing.
Supports claim with logical reasoning and evidence	The piece strongly supports the claim with logical reasoning and relevant evidence, using 3–5 accurate, credible sources, and demonstrating a thorough understanding of the topic.	The piece supports the claim with logical reasoning and relevant evidence, using 3–5 accurate, credible sources, and demonstrating an understanding of the topic.	The piece supports the claim, though at times not clearly, with some reasons and evidence, using 1–2 sources.	The piece does not support claim with logical reasoning and evidence.
Uses words to create cohesion and clarify relationships among the claim, reasons, and evidence	The piece consistently uses words to create cohesion and clarify relationships among the claim, reasons, and evidence.	The piece sometimes uses words to create cohesion and clarify relationships among the claim, reasons, and evidence.	The piece rarely uses words to create cohesion and clarify relationships among a claim, reasons, and evidence.	The piece does not use words to create cohesion and clarify relationships.
Establishes and maintains a formal style	The piece establishes and maintains an engaging and formal style.	The piece establishes and maintains a formal style.	The piece establishes, but inconsistently maintains, a formal style.	The piece does not establish a formal style.
Provides a concluding statement	The conclusion follows from and supports the argument presented in a new and interesting way.	The conclusion follows from and supports the argument presented.	The conclusion only somewhat follows from and supports the argument presented.	The conclusion is not provided.

Written Argument Planning Sheet

Introduction (statement of the issue and stance): _____
_____

Point 1 (paraphrased from source): _____
_____

Source for point 1: _____

Point 2 (paraphrased from source): _____
_____

Source for point 2: _____

Point 3 (paraphrased from source): _____
_____

Source for point 3: _____

Point 4 (paraphrased from source): _____
_____

Source for point 4: _____

Point 5 (paraphrased from source): _____
_____

Source for point 5: _____

Conclusion and restatement of issue and stance: _____
_____
_____

A Reader's Comprehension of the Texts

my notes

This Student Reader is full of information about natural disasters and extreme weather. You will read about different weather-related natural disasters and also about places on Earth with extreme climates. You will learn about those who study natural disasters and extreme weather and what can be done to prepare for them. After all, the more we learn about natural disasters and extreme weather, the better we can protect ourselves.

Writing about what you read is important. That is why this section called "My Notes: A Reader's Comprehension of the Texts"—or just "My Notes"—is here. You will use these note pages to answer short questions, define words, and jot down interesting facts about what you read. The writing you do in My Notes is just for you. It will not be graded or collected, and it is yours to keep.

You will write in My Notes after every reading to practice using new vocabulary and reflect on new ideas. Writing will help you consider how new ideas relate to ideas from past readings. Soon, My Notes will become a record of almost everything you know about natural disasters and extreme weather. Best of all—it's yours! You can use it to prepare for a review, a paper, or a project.

Remember that writing—even taking a simple note—will help you to remember and understand what you read.

Photo: © iStockphoto.com/Veeranat Suwangulrut

lesson 1

My Notes on "What Is a Natural Disaster?"

Refer to pages 1–6 in your Student Reader to help you complete these notes.

1. Difference between a natural disaster and a natural occurrence:

2. Natural disasters can cause:

3. New technology has affected preparedness by:

My Notes on "Extreme Weather Matrix"

Refer to pages 7–9 in your Student Reader to help you complete these notes.

1. Difference between a "warning" and a "watch":

2. Time of year thunderstorms, tornadoes, and hurricanes happen:

3. Memories of how a storm affected you:

lesson 3

My Notes on "Weather vs. Climate"

Refer to pages 11–12 in your Student Reader to help you complete these notes.

1. Weather (definition):

2. Climate (definition):

3. Ways National Climate Data Center's climate data has been used:

lesson 4

My Notes on "Tornado!"

Refer to pages 25–28 in your Student Reader to help you complete these notes.

1. Types of places that provide cover from tornadoes:

2. A tornado warning is issued when:

3. Number of tornadoes that strike the United States each year:

4. Possible reactions people might have while experiencing a tornado:

lesson 5

My Notes on "Tornado!"

Refer to pages 25–28 in your Student Reader to help you complete these notes.

1. Pronoun (definition):

2. Noun substitution (definition):

3. Antecedent (definition):

4. Examples of personal pronouns:

5. Examples of possessive pronouns:

lesson 6

My Notes on "Birth of a Twister"

Refer to pages 31–34 in your Student Reader to help you complete these notes.

1. Wind shear (definition):

2. Location of Tornado Alley:

3. Meaning of appearance of a wall cloud:

4. Reason it is called Tornado Alley:

lesson 7

My Notes on "Unlocking the Whirlwind's Mysteries"

Refer to pages 37–42 in your Student Reader to help you complete these notes.

1. When John Park Finley received meteorological training:

2. Predictions Finley got right in 1884:

3. Reason the U.S. Air Force started studying tornado prediction:

4. Why Fawbush-Miller's prediction was lucky:

5. Change in 1951 regarding tornado predictions:

6. Affect of these events on our society today:

lesson 8

My Notes on "Unlocking the Whirlwind's Mysteries" and "Tornado Scales"

Refer to pages 43–45 in your Student Reader to help you complete these notes.

1. Creator of the Fujita Scale:

2. Reason they rank a tornado based on the damage it causes:

3. Reason Tetsuya Theodore Fujita went to Urbana, Illinois:

4. What Fujita discovered in the data:

5. Affect of discovery on human society:

lesson 9

My Notes on "Recent Natural Disasters"

Refer to pages 49–52 in your Student Reader to help you complete these notes.

1. Deadliest tornado ever recorded:

2. Reason the fires in California spread quickly:

3. How snow increases floodwater:

4. Difference between an implied main idea and an explicit main idea:

5. Why the USGS shifted their focus:

6. Social issues that come with flooding:

lesson 10

My Notes on "Wild Weather" and "Thunderstorm Basics"

Refer to pages 55–62 in your Student Reader to help you complete these notes.

1. Temperature of a bolt of lightning:

2. Lightning conductor (definition) and why they are important:

3. Thunder (definition):

4. Three ingredients required for a thunderstorm to form:

5. Why you should still not go outside during the dissipating stage of a storm:

lesson 11

My Notes on "Hurricanes: The Greatest Storms on Earth"

Refer to pages 67–72 in your Student Reader to help you complete these notes.

1. What the eye is:

2. Why the eye is calm:

3. How the northern side of the storm affects the area it hits:

4. Why or why not rain bands are dangerous:

lesson 12

My Notes on "Hurricanes: The Greatest Storms on Earth"

Refer to pages 67–72 in your Student Reader to help you complete these notes.

1. How storm surge affects the coast:

2. Why storm surge is considered a hurricane's most destructive weapon:

3. The determining factors on the Saffir-Simpson Scale:

4. Number of categories on the Saffir-Simpson Scale:

5. The difference between a Category 4 and a Category 5 hurricane:

lesson 13

My Notes on "Hurricane Hazards"

Refer to pages 77–81 in your Student Reader to help you complete these notes.

1. Possible affects of a category 3 hurricane on a city:

2. Number of tropical storms on average form in the Atlantic Ocean, Caribbean Sea, and Gulf of Mexico each year:

3. Kind of damage a storm surge can cause:

4. Inland flooding (explanation):

5. Possible affect of inland flooding on society:

lesson 14

My Notes on "Can Anyone Stop the Waves?"

Refer to pages 83–86 in your Student Reader to help you complete these notes.

1. Floating breakwater (definition):

2. How these breakwaters could affect society if they were used all along the coast:

3. Venice, Italy's major issue:

4. How floating breakwaters work:

lesson 15

My Notes on "Chasing the Storm"

Refer to pages 89–92 in your Student Reader to help you complete these notes.

1. What the 53rd Weather Reconnaissance Squadron does for the United States:

2. How "Hurricane Hunters" help reduce the cost of evacuation:

3. Cause of flooding in New Orleans during Katrina in 2005:

4. How modern forecasting has saved lives:

5. How non-coastal areas can be affected by hurricanes:

lesson 16

My Notes on "Hurricane Hunters" and "Restore Vital Hurricane Hunters Aircraft Operations"

Refer to pages 95–99 in your Student Reader to help you complete these notes.

1. Why Hurricane Hunters fly into hurricanes:

2. Notes or questions about the video:

3. Why Congresswoman Castor wrote letter:

4. Reasons for restoring funding to Hurricane Hunters Aircraft Operations budget:

lessons 17-18

My Notes on Library Research

Refer to pages 101–104 in your Student Reader to help you complete these notes.

1. Evaluate the reliability of websites you visited:

2. Favorite presentation and why:

3. Additional notes or questions about presentations:

lesson 19

My Notes on "Coldest Place—Antarctica" and "Hottest Temperature—El Azizia, Libya"

Refer to pages 105–113 in your Student Reader to help you complete these notes.

1. Desert (definition):

2. How society benefits from scientific study in these deserts:

3. How both places can be deserts when they have drastically different temperatures:

4. Why scientists can only stay in Antarctica for a short time:

lesson 20

My Notes on "Atacama Desert—The World's Driest Desert" and "Wettest Place—Cherrapunji, India"

Refer to pages 115–118 in your Student Reader to help you complete these notes.

1. What scientists use the Atacama Desert for:

2. When humans started keeping records of temperatures in the Atacama Desert:

3. How the Atacama Desert is helpful to the film world:

4. How monsoons affect Cherrapunji, India:

lesson 21

My Notes on "Death Valley Weather and Climate"

Refer to pages 121–129 in your Student Reader to help you complete these notes.

1. This makes Death Valley so extreme:

2. How Death Valley compares with other deserts:

3. How "rainshadow" affects Death Valley:

4. How heat gets trapped by the valley's depths in Death Valley:

lesson 22

My Notes on "Death Valley Weather and Climate"

Refer to pages 121–129 in your Student Reader to help you complete these notes.

1. How water affects the land it runs through:

2. Benefit of studying the rocks in Death Valley:

3. Affects of volcanoes we can see in Death Valley:

4. What the "pulling apart" of Earth's crust allows:

My Notes on "The Dust Bowl"

Refer to pages 133–140 in your Student Reader to help you complete these notes.

1. How humans affected the drought:

2. How dust storms in the middle of the country affected people on the East Coast:

3. Affect of dust storms on education:

4. Explain Black Sunday:

lesson 24

My Notes on "China's Growing Deserts Are Suffocating Korea"

Refer to pages 143–147 in your Student Reader to help you complete these notes.

1. Social effects of dust storms:

2. Steps to help reduce dust storms:

3. Country or countries causing the dust storms in Asia:

lesson 25

My Notes on "Blizzard of 1966"

Refer to pages 149–151 in your Student Reader to help you complete these notes.

1. Reason the blizzard of 1966 resulted in greater amounts of snow near Oswego:

2. Transportation problems can arise from severe weather, causing problems such as:

3. Ways in which Syracuse would be better prepared to deal with similarly large amounts of snow today:

4. How multimedia enriches a written text:

lesson 26

My Notes on "Winter Storms: The Deceptive Killers"

Refer to pages 153–168 in your Student Reader to help you complete these notes.

1. Dangers of winter storms:

2. Affects blizzards can have on cities:

3. How winter flooding causes problems for cities that are built on rivers:

4. The most important thing for surviving hypothermia if medical care is not available:

5. Three elements needed for a winter storm:

lesson 27

My Notes on "Winter Storms: The Deceptive Killers"

Refer to pages 153–168 in your Student Reader to help you complete these notes.

1. Why you need a battery-powered NOAA Weather Radio:

2. Examples of items you should have before a winter storm strikes in order to be prepared:

3. What to do when caught inside during a winter storm and you don't have heat:

4. Steps for making a family disaster plan:

lesson 28

My Notes on "Climate Change Basics"

Refer to pages 171–181 in your Student Reader to help you complete these notes.

1. Role of greenhouse effect on Earth:

2. Role of greenhouse gases on Earth:

3. How humans affect climate change:

4. How the landscape of Earth affects the weather:

lesson 29

My Notes on "Climate Change Basics"

Refer to pages 171–181 in your Student Reader to help you complete these notes.

1. Particulate matter (definition and danger):

2. How plants and animals use carbon:

3. Cause of global warming:

4. Impact of volcanic eruptions on atmosphere:

lesson 30

My Notes on the Culminating Project

Use this extra space to jot down ideas or take notes while planning your project.

Credits

Grateful acknowledgement is made to the following for copyrighted material:

Carus Publishing Company
"Can Anyone Stop the Waves?" by Nick D'Alto from *Odyssey* issue: Surf's Up! © 2006 Carus Publishing Company, published by Cobblestone Publishing, 30 Grove Street, Suite C, Peterborough, NH 03458. All Rights Reserved. Used by permission of the publisher.

DOGO MEDIA, INC.
"Atacama Desert—The World's Driest Desert" by Meera Dolasia from www.dogonews.com. Used by permission.

Dorling Kindersley Publishing, Inc.
"Wild Weather" (p. 34) from *Eyewitness: Natural Disasters* by Claire Watts and Trevor Day (Dorling Kindersley 2006). Copyright © Dorling Kindersley Limited, 2006. Used by permission.

Extreme Science
"Coldest Place—Antarctica" and "Hottest Temperature—El Azizia, Libya" from www.extremescience.com. Used by permission of Extreme Science.

Ganzel Group
"The Dust Bowl" by Bill Ganzel from Drought, adapted from the Wessels Living History Farm Web site, http://www.livinghistoryfarm.org. Used by permission.

Millbrook Press
"Tornado!" "Birth of a Twister," and "Unlocking the Whirlwind's Mysteries" by Laurie Lindop from *Chasing Tornadoes*. Used by permission.

National Oceanic and Atmospheric Administration (NOAA)
"Enhanced F Scale for Tornado Damage" from www.spc.noaa.gov/faq/tornado/ef-scale.html, "Thunderstorm Basics" from www.nssl.noaa.gov/primer/tstorm/tst_basics.html, "Record Tornadoes" from www.noaanews.noaa.gov/2011_tornado_information.html, "Winter Storms: The Deceptive Killers" from www.weather.gov/om/winter/resources/Winter_Storms2008.pdf, "Extreme Weather Matrix" from www.noaawatch.gov/themes/tropical.php and http://www.noaawatch.gov/themes/severe.php, "Saffir-Simpson Scale" from http://www.aoml.noaa.gov/general/lib/laescae.html, "Tornado Alley" from www.nssl.noaa.gov/primer/tornado/tor_climatology.html#, "The Blizzard of '66 and Lake Effect Snow" from www.erh.noaa.gov/aly/Past/WINTER.htm and http://docs.lib.noaa.gov/rescue/mwr/094/mwr-09-04-0275.pdf, "Wildfires in the West" from http://earthobservatory.nasa.gov/IOTD/view.php?id=8148, "Weather vs. Climate" from www.ncdc.noaa.gov and http://oceanservice.noaa.gov, and "Hurricane Hunters" from http://oceantoday.noaa.gov/hurricanehunters/.

Storm2K
"Wettest Place—Cherrapunji, India" from www.storm2k.org. Used by permission.

WTVH
"Blizzard Of 1966, Syracuse, NY: Ron Remembers." Used by permission.

The New York Times Company
"China's Growing Deserts Are Suffocating Korea" by Howard W. French from *The New York Times*, 4/14/2002 issue © 2002 The New York Times. All rights reserved. Used by permission and protected by the Copyright Laws of the United States. The printing, copying, redistribution, or retransmission of this Content without express written permission is prohibited.

Tornado Project Online
"Fujita Scale": Used by permission of the Tornado Project.

U.S. Geological Survey
"Record Floods" and "Global Reach of Volcanic Gases" from the U.S. Geological Survey, Department of the Interior/USGS.

Windows to the Universe
"Tornado Scales," "Hurricane Damage," and "Chasing the Storm": The source of this material is Windows to the Universe, at http://www.windows2universe.org/ at the National Earth Science Teachers Association (NESTA). Windows to the Universe® is a registered trademark. All Rights Reserved.

Note: Every effort has been made to locate the copyright owner of material reproduced in this component. Omissions brought to our attention will be corrected in subsequent editions.